MEDIEVAL LITERATURE
AND CULTURE

Andrew Galloway

continuum

Continuum

The Tower Building
11 York Road
London SE1 7NX

80 Maiden Lane
Suite 704
New York, NY 10038

www.continuumbooks.com

First published 2006
Reprinted 2008

British Library Cataloguing-in-Publication Data
A catalogue record for this book is available from the British Library.

ISBN 10: 0-8264-8656-8 (hardback)
          0-8264-8657-6 (paperback)

ISBN 13: 978-08264-8656-1 (hardback)
          978-08264-8657-8 (paperback)

Typeset by Servis Filmsetting Ltd, Manchester
Printed and bound in Great Britain by MPG Books Ltd, Bodmin, Cornwall

MEDIEVAL LITERATURE AND CULTURE

INTRODUCTIONS TO BRITISH LITERATURE AND CULTURE SERIES

Introductions to British Literature and Culture are practical guides to key literary periods. Guides in the series are designed to help introduce a new module or area of study, providing concise information on the historical, literary and critical contexts and acting as an initial map of the knowledge needed to study the literature and culture of a specific period. Each guide includes an overview of the historical period, intellectual contexts, major genres, critical approaches and a guide to original research and resource materials in the area, enabling students to progress confidently to further study.

FORTHCOMING TITLES

Renaissance Literature and Culture by Lisa Hopkins and Matthew Steggle

Seventeenth-Century Literature and Culture by Jim Daems

Eighteenth-Century Literature and Culture by Paul Goring

Romanticism by Sharon Ruston

Victorian Literature and Culture by Maureen Moran

Modernism by Leigh Wilson

Postwar British Literature and Culture 1945–1980 by Susan Brook

Contemporary British Literature and Culture by Sean Matthews

Contents

Introduction

Sometimes scholars say that medieval culture has no sense of history – that its perspective is timeless, reduced to a continuous 'present', lacking the dimensions and 'perspective' said to have emerged with the Renaissance, not to mention the sense of an individual self, an idea of authorship, and a notion of a unified, bureaucratic state. In fact, scholars and non-scholars alike more often mention the Middle Ages in terms of what it isn't than what it is: either the detritus of the Roman empire, or the unassembled pieces of the modern age. A recent essay in a respected journal on international politics – surveying the rise of 'gang-controlled communities in Jamaica' and other developing countries, the growth of multinational corporations and the increasing entwining of major cities to other international cities more closely than to anything nearby – declares that we are entering a 'New Middle Ages', since the integrity of the modern state, the writer believes, is disintegrating on every side. The historical parallel – appearing more than a few times during the last quarter century – is provocative. But it has serious limits. One is that the image it offers for 'the Middle Ages' easily ends up as a luridly 'primitive' and quasi-tribal tableau: 'the [Jamaican] gangs demonstrate, almost celebrate, their independence and defiance of authority at raucous late-night dances patrolled by local cadres. Such warlordism would have been familiar to the western Europeans of a millennium ago' (J. Rapley, 'The new Middle Ages', *Foreign Affairs* 85(3), May/June 2006: 95–103 (100)).

Perhaps. But perhaps our willingness to lump together nearly a thousand years – from, say, the arrival of Christianity to the Anglo-Saxons in 597, to the dissolution of the medieval church in England in the 1530s – and to distill a vast and (like all cultural configurations, including Jamaican gangs) intricate and sophisticated number of coexisting cultural worlds into a single moment shows that it is we who have no sense of history.

Even a slightly closer look dispels many of the generalizations about the Middle Ages that we commonly make or imply. To start with, our view of a medieval lack of historical vision is quite wrong. Understanding medieval literature requires a very respectful investigation of how visions of history bring the past and the present into complex relationships with each other on anything but a simple, flat plane – as a reading of *Beowulf* (? *c.* 800), Chaucer's *Troilus and Criseyde* (*c.* 1386), or indeed any part of the vast tradition of medieval historical literature and historical writing shows. The other topics associated with the Renaissance and modernity just mentioned have medieval forms too, some of which will be noted in the following chapters. They are often different from ours, but our inability to grasp them except as shattered or formative versions of something that we understand better – on their way from or to some more monumental period and point of society (Rome, or us) – does not justify giving up in the effort to understand them in themselves.

Divisions in history are necessary for organizing understanding, and there is no denying that Western culture and its literature were profoundly different from ours in the period between fifteen hundred and six hundred years ago in what we now call England. Indeed, one measure of that is in the shaping of time and of the modes of communication (always closely related things, and both clearly important for the nature of literature, historical understanding and many other aspects of life). Whereas we often exist in a world of up-to-the-minute but endlessly recycled and commercially supported global reports, in print but more often continuously transmitted digital images, from which we step away in our often minutely scheduled lives to consume in silence (if we do) written prose or poetry that has been reproduced in many identical copies – or, more often, to watch and listen to hyper-realistic enactments of stories also circulated in exact digital replicas – in contrast, the culture in England reaching back nearly a millennium before the age of printing, public clocks and the crown's supreme control of the English church relied on frequent and methodically timed collective worship, ritual and entertainment, which followed the seasons and whose patterns changed only rarely and usually gradually. Its stories were uncontrollably shared, elaborated and compiled, including historically essential ones as well as morally edifying or completely unedifying ones, all of whose crafted but ever-changing features were manifested in unwritten memory as often as in individually hand-written documents that, vast and deeply sophisticated, or brief and ephemeral as they might be, were all unique, meant to be read aloud and fully decipherable, for most of this span, by only a minority of the population, most of whom had a lifelong religious profession.

Its features are alien indeed – and 'they' might say the same thing about 'us'. Yet that span of culture has left its traces everywhere, certainly in university life and its innovations: from how we index books and organize their parts (a thirteenth-century invention), to how we think about 'rights', social obligations, or political representation. The difficulty of summing up any period may be a good thing for it, but in this case it has tended to leave it rather a blur, a foil to everything before and after, one often assumed to be somehow lacking the sharper elements of human consciousness, inventiveness and sense of justice and ethics (the 'flat sense of history' again). These views are often quite ironically wrong. There are few periods in human history, for instance, when ethics was as intently and universally pondered and emphasized – not ancient Rome; arguably not the humanist Renaissance either. Yet in modern slang and modern policy journals, 'medieval' is generally a deeply pejorative word.

We can certainly find in medieval culture the founding elements of the idea of 'literature' as a serious, immensely intellectually fruitful object of vigorous commentary, applied at least to some kind of narrative and poetry. The long medieval tradition of highly focused and energetic textual interpretation reaches from the monastic contemplation of the *sacra pagina*, the 'sacred page' (i.e. the Bible), to the more elaborate modes of analysis and commentary fostered in the universities (themselves invented in this period) from the thirteenth century on, often framing or surrounding texts with a ring of a standard or 'ordinary' gloss, then a further concentric ring or partial ring of commentary upon that. Such glossing was originally applied only to the Bible and to texts of civil and canon law, but later also to a wide array of classical and even some contemporary medieval literature, in Latin especially, but also French and, elsewhere in Europe, Italian. In a few cases, in the late medieval period, Latin glosses are applied to English works too. At least a few copies of the anonymous English poem for confessors, the *Pricke of Conscience* – the most popular English poem of the Middle Ages, but hardly read in the modern world – have elaborate Latin commentaries around the English verse (e.g. the copy in Brussels, Bibliothèque royale, MS IV 998). All our copies of Chaucer's longer writings have some Latin glosses, some lengthy, although these are absent from any modern student copies. The secular poet John Gower, Chaucer's friend, seems responsible for the extensive Latin glosses found around the English verses of his long poem, the 'Lover's Confession' (*Confessio Amantis*), although it is not certain how much serious guidance we should take from those.

Even when medieval literature lacks such a visible framework of interpretive labor, its treatment and presentation, by authors as well as those who read it, directly founds our view of literary works as objects worthy of careful scrutiny and critical discussion. Medieval writers were often more adept than we realize in anticipating and incorporating into their works comments on or hints to their own thematic and intellectual possibilities. Such self-consciousness and sophistication are central to its general literary and cultural achievement.

Seeing medieval culture as the chief 'alternative' world to what is familiar, however, has a long lineage, one imbedded in its name. The Middle Ages as a named 'period' was made familiar by learned and imaginative early seventeenth-century antiquarians, such as William Camden. Like others in his period, Camden saw the ancient world of Greece and Rome as the first blaze of literature and civilization, rekindled only in his own time, 'this our learned age' (*Certain Poemes* . . ., in *Remaines of a Greater Worke* [1605]). The term 'Renaissance' became widely used in the sixteenth and seventeenth centuries, as in the writings of the Italian painter Giorgio Vasari, who viewed the paintings of Cimabue and Giotto as marking the beginning of the *rinascita dell'arte* that superseded a millennium of darkness and barbarism.

In these visions of history's drama, the role of the ages 'in between' is as something quite different from what 'we' are and what the ancient world was – yet remarkably undefined in itself, in contrast to the Classical Period, the Renaissance or Modernity, all of whose names have something distinctive, monumental and imperial about them (and all of which stand in closer alignment with one another than any does with the period in the 'middle'). Perhaps for this reason, the term 'medieval' or 'Middle Ages' (and only English has that phrase in the plural, offering a useful opportunity to pursue its diversity) has come in recent years to be replaced with 'premodern'. That term is indeed evocative, but its implications should not go unchallenged. 'Premodern' defines a boundless period, visible simply as contrast to, and perhaps prelude to, the line of the present, 'modern' (or 'Early Modern') world. The label 'premodern' was coined to avoid the storybook sense of history as having a 'beginning, middle, and [triumphant finale] present'. But it can also imply a simplistic notion of what 'we' are as well as what 'they' were. It is simply everything 'pre' us, which logically might include the Bronze Age as easily as Shakespeare's Catholic father.

'Premodern' may even contribute to – although the scholars who use it embody the opposite impulse – a general loss of deep historical understanding or historical questioning. For 'premodern' implies an inevitable teleology at least as clearly as 'medieval' or 'middle'. With 'premodern', history's unpredictable causes may seem less important, replaced by a hint of the inevitable growth of a single organic being. The widespread developments in history that come crashing into more or less cohesive cultures from the four-teenth through the sixteenth centuries, with vastly trans-forming effects – from microbes of a plague in the mid-fourteenth century that killed perhaps a third of the population, especially the laboring classes who swiftly became a scarcer (and somewhat more politically potent) entity, to the discovery of vast sums of gold in the New World in the early sixteenth, which led to economic volatility and a shift to a monetary economy on a scale never before experi-enced, to the host of other chance events that keep history from ever being a tidy syllogism based on pre-established terms – are minimized with 'pre-', as if the 'modern' period that emerged were a butterfly emerging from a chrysalis, or a young adult from a pre-adolescent. Chaucer's partial hints of 'wry, ironic self-fashioning' are then seen as the faltering steps toward the Renaissance's full-fledged self-fashioning, which is thus worthier of direct attention.

More pertinent to a survey of 'medieval English litera-ture', scholarship that addresses 'premodern' literature tends to find its focus just a short distance behind 'early Modern' (i.e. sixteenth- and seventeenth-century) literature, not back further in the preceding millennium. Thus in practice, 'pre-modern' scholarship often means writing on Geoffrey Chaucer (c.1340–1400), or John Lydgate (c.1370–1449), not *Beowulf* or *Judith* (c.900) or Layamon's *Brut* (c.1220). Those are left for other, implicitly more 'traditional' kinds of scholar-ship, and easily dismissed altogether.

This narrowing should be resisted. 'Middle Ages' at least encompasses the whole span. So too, 'medieval English' includes all the materials generally taught in various classes as 'Old' and 'Middle' English – that is, the writing in English recorded from as early as AD 700 through that recorded into the fifteenth century, when many of the language's features began to shift fairly swiftly toward the modern forms. In spite of the transforming effects of the Norman Conquest of 1066, the division between these stretches of English is far less clear, and much more interesting, than the modern scholarly isolation of 'Old English literature' from what followed might suggest. Both 'phases' deserve attention, and they and their cultural contexts should be at least introduced together. This guide has therefore avoided using the common linguistic terms 'Old English', 'early Middle English' and 'Middle English' to define the writings, in favour of simply 'English literature', further specified in terms of its political and cultural period: Anglo-Saxon England, Anglo-Norman England, and later medieval England (these periods are further defined in Chapter 1).

To be sure, the English language assumed an extraordinary variety of forms across this span, some mutually incomprehensible to natives living at the same time at opposite ends of the country, and all displaying sometimes gradual, sometimes more rapid fundamental change. Some details about these changes are presented in Chapter 2, but it is useful to offer here a summary of the phases of the language, along with a crude sketch of the literature's developments.

In the most fully recorded tradition of English poetry in Anglo-Saxon England, under the royal house of the ultimately dominant West Saxons, the language attained a kind of 'standard' status, whose stylistic properties in the written and oral forms produced in and for aristocratic, religious culture were respectfully maintained probably for centuries, though leaving the spoken forms drifting further away from the classical written language. It is worth noting here that the presence of English poetry written down from so early in this period – found in datable forms from the eighth century, and in fairly copious quantities in several large collections made in the later tenth – is extraordinary. No other 'vernacular' (that is, not Latin, the official tongue of ideas, records, theology and government for almost all of the Middle Ages) European language can compare with this precocity. The written language displays its most fundamental changes only when it finally loses its strongest cultural reasons to maintain the standard structures that had inhibited the spoken and regional forms from transforming the written tongue. In 1066, the

French-speaking Normans destroyed the Anglo-Saxon armies of King Harold (who, the Norman duke, William the Bastard, claimed, or had propagandists shrewd enough to claim, had promised William the throne – when, according to one chronicler, William rescued Harold after Harold's boat drifted away during a drinking party and pirates captured him in Normandy [William of Malmesbury, *Gesta regum Anglorum: The History of the English Kings*, ed. and trans. R. A. B. Mynors, R. M. Thomson and M. Winterbottom. Oxford: Clarendon Press 1998, 2.228; vol. 1, 419]). From that point, the ecclesiastical, government and land-owning positions of England – the traditional sources of literary patronage – rapidly shifted into French-speaking hands.

When the Norman Conquest of 1066 removed the aristocratic patronage for the earlier English kinds of poetry, the English that reemerged seems fairly dramatically different, but its changes began simply as the recording of aspects of pronunciation that had long been spoken, and whose features now were able to push over some structures of the formal written language. When English is visible in this period – as it is in a few continued chronicles from Anglo-Saxon traditions, and then in long works again, by the early thirteenth century (with Layamon's *Brut*) and in the mid-thirteenth century with a succession of romances translated and elaborated (like Layamon's work) from French sources – it is a rather different language, or rather range of languages. It presents a remarkably diverse literary and dialectical range, with a generally humble, often ecclesiastical base of support, until shortly after the 'age of Chaucer', when support for English writing begins again to flow from the crown, which pressed into service the kind of English produced in Chancery, the king's writing office, as a new standard for the language.

In what sense, then, is English writing either before or after the Conquest fully definable as an 'English literary tradition'? If English writing before the Conquest, which at least had a dense oral and written tradition, is not recognizable as 'English' to most modern readers (or most English readers two hundred years after the Conquest), the English literature written after the Conquest is continually in the shadow of French; only at the very end of the medieval period does it labor with much sense of an important set of preceding English written works. Neither before nor after the Conquest does English writing offer, in the main, 'literature' in the senses that readers who know only the modern novel or poem might expect. Biblical and extra-biblical religious stories abound in Anglo-Saxon English writing (albeit fully re-imagined, in what we might briefly but inadequately call heroic, Germanic terms); homilies and a few major histories dominate the prose. All are magnificent and fascinating, but all raise questions about just what we expect by 'literature': if it is an account beholden to no agenda, 'art for art's sake', then the more or less clear Christian agenda of most of this writing would disqualify it.

After the Norman Conquest, and until the sixteenth century, the diverse career of recorded English allows for more materials that we might more or less comfortably call 'literary', but even here the bulk of such writing is not that, at least in our terms. It is dominated, similarly, by religious instruction, narratives of saints' lives, prose and verse chronicles of England (candidates for epic status as some, like Layamon's *Brut*, might be), debate poetry and other kinds of lyrics, and aristocratic romances based on French ones.

Only in the last decades of the fourteenth century, with the period of Chaucer and his contemporaries, does a set of non-clerical, worldly, yet intellectually and ethically provocative works appear. But this is a remarkable phenomenon worth studying in itself, not a norm to be expected. These ambitious and original projects purport to offer something like universal histories or inclusive encyclopedias, yet in them the dilemmas and ironies of the present narrator or narrators are as much the point as the broader narratives and issues. This is followed by still heavier production of English writing in the fifteenth century, in works that may be unsettled surveys of the writer's own life (as in Thomas Hoccleve) or long verse histories (as in John Lydgate, treating antiquity, the destruction of Thebes or of Troy, the latter of whose exiles were seen as the ancestors of England's first inhabitants), and it now includes abundant texts of historical and moral drama (if sometimes at the same time explicitly anachronistic, and wryly immoral). All this is accompanied by quantities of religious lyrics, which find ingenious strategies to persuade to piety, human empathy and human love – and which are thus linked to the increasing quantities of secular love lyrics.

'Tradition' – another difficult word in that phrase above – has to be emphasized and scrutinized in special terms too. When we speak in general of the 'English literary tradition', we usually conceive a sense of a burden of written earlier materials that an author must struggle to climb out from under; but for English writers in Anglo-Saxon England, the notion of 'tradition' would almost always mean a mostly unwritten, and entirely declaimed (maybe even regularly sung) context of highly formal phrases and perhaps scenes and plot-lines, whose power a given writer would generally seek to invoke, so long as it could be applied to an ultimately Christian purpose. In the centuries after the Norman Conquest, we may postulate a less rigorously maintained tradition of oral poetry (whose makers were far less exalted homilists and entertainers than they had been in the Anglo-Saxon period), but a generally heavier dependence on writings in other languages: French and, especially by the fourteenth and fifteenth centuries, Latin. Medieval English literature does not depend on, or indeed feel burdened by, earlier written literature in English until a late stage in this span, especially in the fifteenth century, when responding to Chaucer became one of the gambits of nearly all English poets.

Medieval culture and literature are indeed absorbingly distinctive, although also extraordinarily varied and dynamic. Grasping all this is not a matter of a single word, no matter how carefully chosen. It requires exploring a wide range of cultural contexts and historical developments even to begin to see how the elements and traditions of narrative and 'literary' materials formed and interacted. It is useful to start with an introduction to that culture and history.

1

Political, Intellectual and Cultural Contexts

PERIODS, POPULATIONS AND SOCIAL ORDERS

It is difficult by any means to encompass the history of England from the earliest period of Cædmon's 'Hymn' (*c*.680), King Alfred's translations (*c*.890), *Beowulf* (? ninth century) and Wulfstan's *Sermon of the Wulf* (*c*.1014), to the period of the works of Geoffrey Chaucer (d. 1400), William Langland (*c*.1385) and John Lydgate (d. 1449), and of drama like *Mankind* (*c*.1465). For a short overview of this long and wide span of historical and cultural contexts of medieval English literature, it seems best to combine chronology with some persisting social divisions and cultural elements.

The chronology can be carved up into a simple set of large 'period' divisions. To be sure, the elements of these periods and their complex transitions remain matters of endless exploration and debate, but these are common starting points for most historical discussions of medieval England.

First we can identify Roman Britain, which can be said to span from the first century through the early fifth, followed by the Germanic invasions in the fifth and sixth centuries. Next, Anglo-Saxon England encompasses the rule of the

Anglo-Saxon kings from the seventh century to the Norman Conquest in 1066. Anglo-Norman England, with its Norman kings and continental intelligentsia, can be named and plotted from the Conquest through the twelfth century and beyond. Later medieval England, the thirteenth through the fifteenth centuries, offers no other obvious politically or culturally precise label, but these centuries were when much of what we may think of as 'medieval' was most widely in evidence: splendid and central royal courts; knights; love-poetry; friars; public sermons; vigorous academic debate; regular religious feasts and fasts; towering cathedrals; heresy; and plague, unfolding within the wide agrarian expanses of a world that depended on the labor of peasants and laborers, independent and dependent, free and servile, who so rarely figure within our view of this world except for an occasional rebellion, but whose legal and social transformations helped eventually to redefine it.

Before marking any other divisions, it is helpful to gain a sense of the population as a whole. The main portion of the island that is now England, Scotland and Wales was never densely populated, as it could not be given its heavy reliance on an agricultural base. At the coming of the Normans in 1066, Anglo-Saxon England contained possibly two million inhabitants. At the height of its medieval population numbers, in the thirteenth century – at which point England hardly seemed an island, so often did its realm reach into the Continent – its numbers in England alone reached somewhere between four and six million (it is difficult to be precise, because the very few surveys from which this is extrapolated measure only heads of households, and many of those would have evaded tax surveys). Population did not reach this number again until nearly the eighteenth century. The first decades of the fourteenth century were particularly low points: evidence from contraction of fields, from a sudden spike in grain prices, from increasing ages of marriage and from accounts in chronicles all suggest a population collapse, probably mostly due to famine from very poor harvests but also from changes in social options, family timing and other elusive factors responding to constraints on food and usable or available land. Soon after that are many signs of a very precipitous further drop, perhaps a third or even half the population, because of the plague that first arrived from the Levant in 1349, killing a generation of notable intellectuals and writers, among so many others. Plague returned most powerfully in 1361, 1369 (killing John of Gaunt's wife Blanche, commemorated soon after in Chaucer's *Book of the Duchess*) and 1375.

A continued downward reproductive trend followed, reducing the population still further. By the mid-fifteenth century England once again had probably fewer than two million inhabitants. Many fifteenth-century towns and cities proclaimed that they were losing inhabitants drastically; and, although some of the complaints were motivated by obvious efforts to get aid from the king, the physical evidence of deserted or shrunken towns is clear. We may be conscious of the extraordinarily important and ambitious literary and other projects of later fourteenth- and fifteenth-century England, but by the early sixteenth century, the population was not much larger than it had been at the Norman Conquest.

The majority of the population was on the land, which produced the bulk of economic activity, especially in sheep-raising and ploughing. Towns and cities were, in fact, never the centres of population that we think of today. London varied between 30,000 and 70,000 inhabitants (compare perhaps 200,000 for thirteenth-century Paris, and 100,000 for Florence), but very few other English cities ever reached 10,000, and all opened out onto long roads past wide fields, clusters of cottages, manor houses, small parish churches, large stone monasteries and larger stone castles. Most people lived in these non-urban areas.

In spite of this complexity and its chronological duration, a rather stable theory of social division appears throughout much of the whole expanse: the division and interdependence of three 'estates'. The monk and priest Ælfric, in his early eleventh-century English treatise 'On the Old and New

Testaments' (dedicated to a lay lord), compared society's support of the king to a royal throne with three legs:

> *laboratores* [those who work] . . . are those who secure for us the means of subsistence; *oratores* [those who pray] . . . are those who intercede for us with God and . . . serve God through spiritual labor; *bellatores* [those who fight] are those who guard our strongholds . . . engaging in armed combat with any enemy who might invade it . . . On these three legs stands the throne. If one is broken, then immediately the other legs suffer injury.
>
> (*De vetero et novo testamento*; Crawford [1969]: 71)

By the late fourteenth century, a widely copied sermon by the preacher Thomas Wimbledon (*c.*1388) was still declaring the need for all 'three estates', and the principles structure Chaucer's *General Prologue* (*c.*1390) or Langland's Prologue to *Piers Plowman* (*c.*1370–90) only slightly less obviously than they do John Gower's Prologue to the *Confessio Amantis* (*c.*1390) – to name just the most ambitious English writers at the end of the period in question. By this time, the theory of 'three estates' was fairly archaic, at least in its evasion of the emergence (from the twelfth century) of socially prominent merchants and a plethora of specialized urban trades, as well as what we would call professions such as law and medicine (both emerging in the twelfth and thirteenth centuries). That the fourteenth-century poets just mentioned are themselves courtly or urban intellectual laborers who do not easily fit into the 'three estates' is proof of how far English society had developed away from that theory by then – as indeed is the range that these writers present of characters who follow urban, professional and less readily classifiable social roles. But that the writers even at that late date continue to use the scheme, greatly distended as it may be in their hands, suggests that it retained a hold on common understanding and indeed reflected a long-lived cultural reality of the basic facets of medieval self-understanding and life. It provides therefore at least a preliminary way to approach the chronology as well as the features of a span that is complex as well as long indeed.

RULERS AND HIGH POLITICS

Both the periods and some of the general qualities of medieval culture can be introduced by sketching the history of 'those who fight', especially kings and rulers. Rulers and warriors, for better or worse, most clearly and abruptly change the broad political and social circumstances of the mass of people, and these allow us immediately to use the broad periods just defined for the 'Middle Ages'.

Roman Britain and the Germanic invasions

Britannia (including the entire largest island that was later divided into England, Wales and Scotland) first appears, flickeringly, in the surviving historical record as an intriguing unknown land facing a restless Roman governor. In late winter 55 BC, Julius Caesar, Governor of Gaul (before taking over Rome as its most dictatorial consul), turned from stifling the rebellions among the continental Germanic peoples and sailed across the narrow *Fretum Gallicum* ('Gallic Channel') toward the western edge of the known world, *Cantium* (Kent): 'for even if there was not enough time for war, still it seemed very useful if he could visit the island and examine its sort of people, terrain, harbors, and entry-points, since all these things were almost entirely unknown to the Gauls' (*De bello gallico* 4.20).

The adventure was brief. Caesar swiftly discovered the British warriors' distinctive taste for fighting in chariots and on horseback; after being ambushed, he destroyed as much of the area as he could and retreated to Gaul with hostages, returning to his more attainable subjugation of the peoples there. A year later he was able to make a slightly longer foray through *Cantium* and points north, passing around a marshy area transected by a large river, the *Tamesis*, that flowed down to the sea. This time, he managed to gain surrenders from a number of the leaders of tribes. But rebellions and political ambitious elsewhere called him away, and Romans did not return for another ten years.

Wherever Caesar had set foot, however, Roman imperial power eventually followed. Within a century *Britannia* had been colonized, invested with roads, was building up native settlements into Roman-style cities and garrisons (including *Londinium* in that marshy plain) and had been brought into the Roman empire. Only over the following three centuries, however, were its unruly, supposedly blue-painted tribes more or less contained and subdued (or simply kept away), and those were likely at any point to rebel in spite of the long earth walls that several Roman emperors, such as Hadrian (in 133), erected around the Roman-controlled area as (mostly symbolic) limits of their territory.

We have no 'English' or proto-Germanic literature preserved from this period, although Caesar (drawing here, however, on earlier Greek travel-writings) claimed that the *Druids* on the continent, among a similar kind of people, were obliged to complete a 20-year apprenticeship memorizing poetry (in Greek, Caesar implausibly says), since they considered it sacrilegious to commit such things to writing (*De bello gallico* 6.13). A hint of the actual intellectual culture of *Britannia* emerges when, via the Romans, Christianity arrived in Britain in the second century, accompanied, as it had been in Rome, with Mithraism and a variety of highly eclectic combinations of Roman and Germanic religions, traces of which are evident in British wall-paintings as well as coins. The Christian apologist Tertullian, writing *c.*200 in Carthage, north Africa, claimed that 'places in Britain inaccessible to the Romans have been subdued by the Christians' (*Adversos Judaeos* 7.5). Perhaps this is mere hyperbole; yet it usefully reminds us that political and military schemes are never the only ways of mapping boundaries or cultural history.

In the third century, the vast Roman empire fissured into the territories of three continually warring emperors and, by the early fifth century, it collapsed at its center altogether (for reasons that are still debated); outlying regions such as Britain were henceforth obliged to fend for themselves. The largest island still had its well-made Roman roads, cites and boundaries, which reached as far north as the Solway Firth and

Tyne; but the island fell from a barely governed Roman province to a mostly non-Christian, and generally ungovernable, region. After the deposition of the last emperor ruling all of Rome in 476 by the Germanic Odoacer, a succession of fierce assaults by Angles, Saxons and other pagan Germanic peoples from the continent drove the Christians still remaining in Britain (who were probably themselves not 'Romans' by birth but converted native Britons) to Ireland, parts of Wales and across the Channel to 'Brittany'. As Gildas says, in a bombastic, highly alliterative Latin treatise written in Wales in probably the sixth century (*De excidio Britaniae*, bk. 1, chap. 23), the British Christians who survived the Saxon invasions 'trusted their lives to the hills, precipitous, menacing and barricaded; to the densest forests; and to the cliffs of the sea coast' (chap. 25). There the British Celts remained even after the Anglo-Saxons themselves were converted to Christianity (which arrived first to them in 597, at Kent).

Anglo-Saxon England

Anglo-Saxon England has a clear end (as a political entity at least) but rather murky beginnings. In his Latin *Ecclesiastical History* (finished in 731), Bede tells the story ('which we have received from our ancestors') of how Pope Gregory the Great, in Rome, conceived the idea of Christianizing the new Germanic inhabitants of England when he saw how handsome some Anglo-Saxons were who had been taken to Rome as slaves. Aptly are they called Angles (*Angli*), he is said to have cried out, because they look like angels (*angelici*). He thought it a shame that 'minds devoid of inward grace should bear so graceful an outward form' (2.1). So he directed Bishop Augustine (not the earlier saint) to bring them into the Christian empire. Apart from its religious framework, his response was not altogether different from that of earlier Roman emperors when those learned of exotic human resources that Rome might harness.

What we call Anglo-Saxon England was from early on politically divided into the territories north and south of the

Humber River: between 'Northumbria' and the southern kingdoms. It seems to have had a kind of federated structure, whose dominant king, found in various kingdoms at different times, was called 'Bretwald'. Bede mentions seven: Ælle (reigned c.477–91), King of the South Saxons; Ceawlin (r. c.560–93), King of the West Saxons; Æthelbert (r. c. 560–616), King of Kent; Rædwald (r. c.590–620), King of East Anglia; and three kings of Northumbria: Edwin (r. c.616–32), Oswald (r. 633–41) and Oswiu (r. 641–70). Two Mercian kings, Æthelbald (r. 716–57) and Offa (r. 757–96), also clearly held a similar supremacy, and the *Anglo-Saxon Chronicle*, founded by the West Saxon royal house, mentions Bretwald Egbert (802–39) as King of the West Saxons.

Bede's Northumbria, whose kings fought continual battles to carve out territory from the Picts, was the dominant cultural and political center in the seventh century. The Northumbrian church drew scholars, artists and monks from Ireland and the continent as far as Italy, and the books written and illustrated show it to have been a magnificent center of culture, thought, art and writing. A strong influence was from Irish monks, although they did not adhere to the Christianity governed by the Rome-centred church with its standardized calendar of holy days and holy saints, and even its mandatory style of shaving the top (rather than the sides) of the head for the monastic 'tonsure' – all of which was officially accepted for the English church at the Council of Whitby (664). The Irish religious were more often pilgrims and solitaries, dressing different and looking different, but Bede describes them from his settled, very Roman-style monastery with considerable admiration and perhaps some envy.

South of Northumbria, the kingdom of the Mercians (from Anglo-Saxon *mearc*, 'border') dominated the entire western and central region of what is now England well into the eighth century. At least one named author, Cynewulf, and the originals of some known poems, can be placed in Mercia during this period; the Mercian king Offa left a rich tradition of stories, as well as a very large wall built c.790 along the Welsh–English boundary in the style of Hadrian's Wall to the north. All the English poetry from this area is known, like nearly all remaining English poetry and other writing before the Norman Conquest, only in the later West Saxon dialect, since this was the culture that most dominated literary and political domains in the later Anglo-Saxon centuries.

The West Saxons were centered on the southeast and southwest, and they began to build a significant dominion in the ninth century under Alfred the Great (r. 871–99) and, especially, his West Saxon successors Ædward (r. 899–925) and Æthelstan (r. 925–39). Alfred overcame regular depredations and crippling attacks by the pagan Vikings who began arriving each spring from 865 to pillage monasteries and towns. Eventually, after an agreement known as the Treaty of Wedmore (878), the Icelandic and Danish invaders agreed to leave Wessex alone, and they divided the country with Alfred along a line roughly from London to Chester, north and east of which became known as the 'Danelaw', where the names of towns ending in Norse suffixes –ham, –tun, or –by still indicate their established presence.

The division of 878 allowed Wessex to incorporate into itself the West Midlands and thus a significant part of the Mercian kingdom. In time the Danelaw was taken back into Wessex hands; with the joint victory of Æthelstan of Wessex and his brother Eadmund of Mercia at the battle of Brunanburh (937), destroying a powerful Norse–Celtic alliance, England achieved the closest thing to national unity in the Anglo-Saxon period.

Alfred's own aspirations were cultural as well as political. Although he may not personally have made all the translations of major medieval Latin Christian works attributed to him – including Boethius's *Consolation of Philosophy*, Gregory the Great's *Pastoral Care*, Augustine's *Soliloquies* and Orosius's *History Against the Pagans* – he clearly exerted strong encouragement over a massive intellectual revival, which he chose to pursue in English (because, he says in the Preface to Gregory's *Pastoral Care*, so few English clerics still knew Latin). He seems to have yearned for something closer to the intellectual, even monastic life than his constant military efforts allowed him.

His preface to the translations of Augustine's *Soliloquies* (*c*.900) humbly uses the metaphors of common labor to describe the act of gathering and reshaping learned materials, and closes with a plaintive description of building a 'house' of culture and learning for his people that he cannot himself fully enjoy:

> I would advise everyone who is strong and has many wagons to direct his steps to that same forest where I cut these props, and to fetch more for himself and to load his wagons with well-cut staves, so that he may weave many elegant walls and put up many splendid houses and so build a fine homestead, and there may live pleasantly and in tranquility both in winter and summer, as I have not yet done.

By the mid-tenth century, the West Saxons had grown into a sophisticated administrative as well as military power. One sign of this is the evidence of regular transformations of coinage throughout England; such currency replacements imply a strong central government and, in turn, would help spread the idea of the king's power and name. The literary evidence is similarly revealing: Wessex monasteries, under royal guidance and patronage, produced literary, historical and theological writings on a uniquely ambitious scale, the first major production of vernacular writing anywhere in Western Europe. Copious production of Latin works followed with the 'Benedictine reform' of the late tenth century, which, under West Saxon rule, sought to regularize the liturgy and increase the level of learning, in Latin and English, at the major cathedral churches of Winchester, Worcester and Canterbury, under the powerful bishops Æthelwold (d. 984), St Oswald (d. 992) and St Dunstan (d. 988).

Both the Latin and the English writing, and the books that preserve them, display high standards and regularity; it is thought that the 'standard English' from this time is in large part the result of the school of Æthelwold at Winchester. Yet the general distinctness and regularity of the formal Anglo-Saxon language probably precedes this. In all of its preserved dialects, for instance, it presents very few loan-words from other tongues. Neither Welsh nor Old Norse, neighbors though they were, left much imprint on its written forms. Only after the Norman Conquest, when the earlier standards for written English have fallen away, are we able to see that English from the Anglo-Saxon period had indeed absorbed words from other cultures, especially Old Norse, which were barred from the formal written language.

To some extent this regularity was probably due to the monastic institutions that fostered such literature from probably its earliest point. Anglo-Saxon literature (discussed in the next chapter) is clearly oriented to a monastic setting and outlook, and consorts readily with early Christian writings that stress the need for detachment from worldly desires and commitments amid a round of prayer and liturgical ritual, and, of course, a deep familiarity with the Bible. Yet such literature also shows that the monks who wrote it down had plenty of contact with aristocratic secular society and its traditions and stories. The *Anglo-Saxon Chronicle* traces the lineage of Cerdic and his son Cynric, the founders of the West Saxons, back to Woden, the supreme god worshipped by the continental Germanic peoples, although he is here treated as an early hero, not a god. The influence of Germanic literature and its gods is clear throughout Anglo-Saxon England, even in its most Christian materials and scenes. In the elaborately carved 'Franks Casket' from eighth-century Northumbria (now in the British Museum), for instance, the violent adventures of Wayland the Smith are incorporated into the Adoration of the Magi.

Late West Saxon and Anglo-Norman England

West Saxon continuity and power were disrupted by the eleventh century. Battles and raids between the Danes and English continued, and in 1013 Svein Forkbeard, king of Denmark, again invaded the kingdom of the West Saxons. Æthelred II 'the unready' (i.e. 'ill-advised'; r. 979–1016) fled to Normandy, leaving the throne available for Svein's son, Cnut, to rule England as well as Denmark (r. 1017–35). Such was the context of the famous 'sermon of the Wulf' by Wulfstan (*c*.1014), with its stark portrayal of the burning and destruction of Christian churches and the murder and exile of the English; such also was the likeliest period for direct influence of Norse poetry, as well as pagan Norse religion, on English culture. A state of near-civil war unfolded between Cnut's offspring and their followers until power was again concentrated in the hands of the saintly and celibate – and thus final – West Saxon king, Edward the Confessor (r. 1047–66). This interval appears idyllic in the later *Life of St Edward*, yet it included continuous rebellions between the major lords vying for a claim to the throne, Tostig and Earl Siward, until Siward's son, Harold II, claimed the throne in 1066. The same year Harold made some oath of support to the Duke of Normandy, William. Perhaps Harold promised William the crown of England; so later Norman and Anglo-Norman chronicles tell, and so too displays the 270-foot long Bayeux Tapestry (*c*.1170), probably made for William's brother Odo as propaganda (intriguingly, however, the tapestry also shows a scene of a Norman soldier torching a home from which a mother and child are fleeing). In any case, Harold denied the oath, and William with a large force of Normans killed him and defeated his army at Hastings in 1066.

The battle itself was not as obviously momentous as, say, the battle of Brunanburh, and in some ways its immediate consequences were no greater than the recent rule over Anglo-Saxon England of a Danish king and his squabbling sons. But thanks to William's more ambitious administrative plans, epitomized by the tabulation of his new country's properties in 'Domesday Book' (1086), the 'Anglo-Norman' period marks a profound disruption over the long term. It imposed Norman clergy, Norman lords and the French tongue on the English; it led to a new kind of imposingly tall, arcaded abbeys with elegant semi-circular arches (the 'Romanesque' style), and a new kind of towering stone castle, replacing the squat churches and fortresses of Anglo-Saxon England. Most of the populace continued to speak their regional dialects of English; a considerable number of clerics continued to copy their most popular English sermons from the Anglo-Saxon period; and most of the previous royal administrators continued for a generation to operate the efficient Anglo-Saxon bureaucracy. But still larger changes soon begin to be evident, in language, government, church, law, and the social hierarchy. Perhaps the most visible change was the concentration of landlordship at the highest level into the hands of a dozen very powerful Norman lords, replacing the hundred or more Anglo-Saxon lords who had been the major landlords of Anglo-Saxon England.

Norman culture did not grant rule automatically to the first-born, and William (r. 1066–87), who remained duke of Normandy as well as king of England, gave England to his middle son, William II (r. 1087–1100), and the duchy of Normandy to his oldest son, Robert. The dual inheritance remained a volatile element throughout medieval English military and political history. When Robert tried to conquer England for himself, this gave William II a good excuse to conquer Normandy back, putting it directly under English rule again. The venture was not completed until their youngest brother Henry I claimed the throne (r. 1100–35), sealing the victory by imprisoning his brother Robert for life.

Since Henry had no son himself, he could only ask his barons to swear an oath of loyalty to let his daughter Matilda be the heiress to the throne; but when Matilda married the ambitious Geoffrey of Anjou the barons rejected their oath. Into the vacuum stepped William I's grandson Stephen, son of William the Conqueror's daughter Adela (r. 1135–54), and thus began England's most divisive and brutal civil war. One branch of the *Anglo-Saxon Chronicle* (branch 'E') was continued through the end of Stephen's reign, and, amid its generally critical view of the Anglo-Normans, it provides under the year 1137 a famous description of the extortion and torments imposed on the common people by the soldiers serving both claimants to the throne:

Both by night and by day they seized those men whom they imagined had any wealth, common men and women, and put

them in prison to get their gold and silver, and tortured them
with unspeakable tortures, for no martyrs were ever tortured as
they were. They hung them up by the feet and smoked them with
foul smoke. They hung them by the thumbs, or by the head, and
hung mail-coats on their feet. . . . Some they put into a 'crucet-
hur' [torture-box], that is, into a chest that was short and narrow
and shallow, and put sharp stones in there and crushed the man
in there . . . In many of the castles was a 'lof and grin' [head-
band and noose], that were chains such that two or three men
had enough to do to carry one. . . . it is fastened to a beam, and
a sharp iron put around the man's throat and his neck so that he
could not move in any direction, neither sit nor lie nor sleep . . .

That the torture-instruments are named in words with
English roots suggests that the lords enacting these horrors
were not simply Normans. That the words require
definitions, however, suggests that they were part of a new
repertoire. In a notably relieved if much briefer entry, the last
writer of the *Anglo-Saxon Chronicle* closes his ancient tradition
with the accession of Matilda's son Henry.

Henry II (r. 1154–89) was a great reformer of English law
and a re-maker of it into newly centralized forms, especially
increasing the use of 'justices in eyre' to travel throughout the
kingdom to transact royal business and assemble a county
court to hear all manner of pleas. His Assize of Clarendon
(1166) established means for inquiring into all crimes
throughout the kingdom, ordered jails to be built in every
shire and codified the procedures that local officials would
use to cooperate with the royal justices. The procedures,
however, could be elaborate and cases could drag on for years
through numerous courts, local and royal. The Assize of
Clarendon also found new uses for the judicial ordeal, the
'trial by water' that would allow God to judge a criminal:
anyone 'accused or notoriously suspected' of robbery,
murder or theft who could not be convicted on other evidence would be subjected to the ordeal. If the water
'rejected' him and he floated, he would undergo mutilation
(loss of a foot, later a hand and a foot); if the water 'accepted'

him, he would be left intact. But even those who passed the ordeal, if known to be 'of ill repute', were forced to abjure the king's lands. God's judgement remained a principle of legal determination even in an age of rapidly increasing royal administration. But public repute, an equally venerable principle of social order, hedged even that.

Later Medieval England

By the twelfth and thirteenth centuries the aristocracy could claim a kind of quasi-religious ideal of 'chivalry', complete with rituals of quasi-baptismal bathing before being dubbed and a ceremonial 'delivery of arms', and celebrated in elaborate tournaments. Much of this is implied in Geoffrey of Monmouth's *History of the Kings of Britain*, 1137, as deriving from the ancient days of King Arthur, the account of whose lineage and power are there first given full expansion. This king, said to rule before the heathen Saxons invaded and destroyed his world, resembles Anglo-Norman kings more than he does Anglo-Saxon ones, and thus his story provides a deeper lineage for the style of Norman culture in England than more obvious (and verifiable) histories could offer – as well as a certain justice to the Norman destruction of the descendants of the Saxons. Apart from the hundreds of copies of Geoffrey's Latin work, the stories proliferated into and became rapidly absorbed by a vast array of chronicles, romances and even royal policies, and certainly reshaped the image of kingship.

The legal, political, and, at least indirectly, literary activity that Henry II inaugurated fit this expanding ideology of chivalry and imperial kingship, as he and his wife Eleanor of Aquitaine established and ruled England's first empire. This comprised not just England and Normandy, but also a continental expanse from Brittany to Aquitaine, bordering on Aragon and Navarre to the south and including Scotland in the north. At the same time, the church also rapidly gained in intellectual, literary, legal and architectural ambition and scale of accomplishment, most visibly in the towering cathedrals of the 'Gothic' style, loftier even than 'Romanesque', that began to be built from 1175 on.

Henry's most famous contribution to political history, however, proceeded from his stubborn adherence to a principle of royal legal authority in opposition to the stubborn adherence to ecclesiastical legal authority by his former chancellor, Archbishop Thomas of Becket. Their opposition spiraled into disaster in 1166 out of an issue that we might see as a question of diplomatic immunity: whether the king's courts had jurisdiction over criminal clerics. Since clerks were governed by Rome, Becket refused to grant to the king's law even this power over them. Becket managed to impose a degree of political paralysis on this extraordinarily ambitious and energetic king, and this led Henry's four chamber knights to take it upon themselves (more or less) to travel to Canterbury and kill the insolent archbishop. During the attack, Becket is said to have adopted a Christlike posture while he knelt at the altar, the ultimate sanctuary for clerical authority. He would have known that his murder meant sanctification, but he could not have guessed how widely and fervently his cult would spread, kept alive by a general populace as well as churchmen eager to insist that the king's powers were not absolute.

The church's massive power and authority was one means, but not the only one, by which English medieval kings' powers were kept in check. To be sure, upholding and enacting the church's ideology could at times strongly bolster royal power and even military action. The king following Henry II, again a middle son, Richard the Lionheart (r. 1189–99), seems to have grasped this point; he spent very little of his reign in England since he was for most of it on Crusade, a massive military endeavor begun a century earlier to 'recapture' the Holy Land from the 'Saracen' infidels. Throughout Christian Europe, the crusades, begun by Pope Urban II in 1095 in response to the Byzantine emperor's call for help against the Turks, joined a literalist religious fervor with an aggressive zeal for war and new territories, drawing in many kings and soldiers. Of English kings only Richard was able fully and personally to commit himself to this endeavor. He died in a minor battle after the Third Crusade, in which he had won the battle of Acre (1191), during which he ordered the execution of thousands of Muslim hostages, including many women and children, because negotiations with the great Muslim ruler, Saladin, had proceeded too slowly.

If anything, this massacre of non-Christians furthered Richard's reputation and prestige, and his literary afterlife; a lurid and fascinating late thirteenth-century English romance, *Richard Coer de Lyon*, based on a lost French one, features his taste for well-cooked Saracen flesh. But in the early thirteenth century, relations with the church helped bring down Richard's brother, King John (1199–1216). John's dispute with the pope led to the king's disgrace and excommunication and to England's long Interdict, when no bodies of laity could be buried with sanctifying rituals, and no masses could be offered to the lay people, who nonetheless were obliged to continue to pay tithes. But political pressures from his higher nobility were more important than the church in John's downfall; his barons, outraged by his dictatorial claims over them, rebelled and demanded a new written guarantee of their rights before the king. He died in political disgrace a year later.

Whatever its original purposes and political crucible, this document, called simply the 'Great Charter' (Magna Carta, 1215), was treasured for its supposed upholding of the 'liberties and rights' of all free men of England – even though only in one chapter (61) appears even a hint that its principles are enforceable by the 'commune of all the land'. That hint is perhaps enough, however, to illuminate (as J. C. Holt argues, 1972: 38–49) how the whole work assumes that England is not a mere possession of the king, but a community of which the king is a single member – a perception long implied but rarely with even this much clarity.

Something of this view continued to be expressed in the growth of parliament, whose roots in the long tradition of a council of the king's higher lords reaches back to the *Witangemot* of late Anglo-Saxon kings. Its largest and most

ceremonial form emerged under the kings following John –
his son Henry III (1216–72) and, especially, his son Edward
I (1272–1307). Yet under these stronger rulers, parliament
mostly served as a means of ratifying the king's will. Only
with the appearance in the mid-fourteenth century of
regular 'petitions' issued to the king by the 'commons' in
parliament – requests that he was forced at least to acknowl-
edge – did parliament represent a significant political check
on the king's power. By the later fourteenth century it was
used twice (1376 and 1388) to impeach close associates of the
king, and in 1399 to depose one. Not coincidentally, the
documents about those unusual late-fourteenth century
parliaments received the fullest attention only during the
seventeenth-century English Revolution.

In many ways, however, the age of a more continuously
volatile balance between king and higher lords began with
John, as is clear during 'the barons' war' of 1258–64 led by
Simon de Montfort against Henry III. From this struggle and
its compromises emerged the first royal proclamation in
English since Anglo-Saxon England, a confirmation of the
'Provisions of Oxford' sent to every shire in England and
Ireland (Dickens and Wilson 1969: 5–9). The appearance of
English as an official language was fleeting, and it was not
firmly established as that until the reign of Henry V
(1414–22), who distributed regular royal letters in English.
But the brief use of English acknowledged the pressures on
royal power from not only a socially elevated community of
French-speaking nobility but also a broader one, even all the
freemen of the realm that Magna Carta mentions.

Henry III's son Edward I, however, behaved as imperial-
istically as such conditions might allow. He imposed his policies firmly on his own lords, and he extended English power
against the neighboring kingdoms of Scotland and, especially, Wales, which he conquered in 1285, establishing for-
midable castles to encircle his control there. Although
Edward did not go on crusade (as he vowed to do when he
was recovering from a serious illness, in 1289), he imposed on
his own country the brutally literal religious 'purification'

that crusade required, expelling all Jews from England in 1290. This certainly did not stop the venerable tradition of anti-Judaic history, literature and drama, but makes its continued popularity somewhat more complicated to assess.

Edward I's idea of England as a firmly royal possession did not survive the disastrous reign of his son, Edward II (1307–27), whose sexual but also deeply fraternal bond to the young Piers Gaveston provided an excuse for a widespread baronial rebellion in 1325, led by the king's wife, Isabella of France, and her lover, Roger Mortimer. Edward II was widely disliked for his absence of military interests or administrative abilities, and he made little effort to maintain the political support that might compensate for this. The story of his terrible death at the hands of his barons in Berkeley Castle may be a popular elaboration that merged a desire to punish his political incompetence with a wish to punish sexual transgressions.

He was but the first of several English kings or heirs in the final two medieval centuries to be assassinated or deposed by other contenders to the throne. Richard II (r. 1378–99), Henry VI (r. 1422–61), Edward V (r. 1483), and Richard III (r. 1483–5) were all victims of such conflicts among and assaults from the higher nobility. Kings who both managed stable reigns and died old in these two centuries were rare indeed: only Edward II's much more militaristic son Edward III (r. 1327–78) fully achieved both. He managed to distract his barons with a long war with France that he waged on the grounds that he was heir to the French crown through his mother, Isabella. His ability to balance the interests of the crown with those of nobility (who profited greatly from the *chevauchées*, or mounted lightning-raids, through French towns) is epitomized by the 'Order of the Garter' that he founded in 1348. This quasi-religious 'order', alluded to in the last line of *Sir Gawain and the Green Knight*, romanticized the war and created a kind of hierarchy of military merit rather than strictly birth – a principle important in a period in which the rise of remarkable individuals above their birth-rank was increasingly common.

Edward III managed to stave off the most humiliating defeats, disadvantageous war treaties and exposure of financial corruption and favoritism among his closest supporters in the court and out until late in his reign; by the time of the 'Good Parliament' of 1376, which invented the legal principle of impeachment in order to condemn an array of his followers, he was senile with age. Perhaps mercifully he was spared full understanding of the death that year of his highly favored son, Edward the Black Prince, as he was oblivious the following year while, as the monastic chronicler Thomas Walsingham reports, his longtime lover Alice Perrers (who herself was convicted in the Good Parliament for abusing royal power) slipped the jeweled rings off his fingers as he died.

Richard II, the son of the Black Prince, had vastly more autocratic dreams but far less political skill and luck. He contended with a succession of parliaments that humiliatingly diminished what he apparently firmly believed to be a royal prerogative to express a dictatorial royal power like the kind currently gaining favor in France. He also contended with a particularly powerful group of barons who happened to be his uncles, the other male sons of Edward III, including John of Gaunt, the most powerful lord in the later Middle Ages. Richard's keen awareness of the battle for royal prerogative took the form of many shrewd legal efforts, such as his emphasis on 'civil law' used on the continent which supported royal power explicitly, rather than the common law of England, whose traditions tended to curb royal power. His style of elegant, continental courtly power carried the seeds of self-destruction in the political environment of England, but it also somehow fostered the most important English writings associated with an English king since the age of Alfred: Chaucer, Gower, possibly the *Pearl* poet, and other writers had direct connections to Richard's volatile and often politically dangerous court. Eventually, in spite of his successful revenge against many of his uncles and their followers, including his probable murder of his uncle Thomas of Woodstock in 1397, Richard had no support left to withstand the claims to the throne by Gaunt's son, Henry Bolingbroke. The show-trial in 1399 for Richard's having sought 'tyrannical' powers to make law as he wanted ended with his imprisonment, and then death (probably by murder) in the Tower, while, as the chronicler Adam Usk reports, Richard lamented the long tradition of English kings who had been 'exiled, slain, destroyed, and ruined' in this 'strange and fickle land' (C. Given-Wilson, *The Chronicle of Adam Usk*. Oxford: Clarendon Press, 1997, pp. 64–5).

The 'Lancastrian' period, beginning with Gaunt, Duke of Lancaster's son, Henry IV (r. 1399–1413), brought into focus issues of a new need not only for royal legitimacy, but also for a new meaning in the war with France. Normandy was once again a goal for reconquest, though this was not achieved during Henry IV's reign. This endured continual rebellions by northern lords, and by the most effective Welsh rebel of the Middle Ages, Owain Glyn Dwr, in 1400–09. Normandy was triumphantly re-conquered in 1415 by Henry IV's son, Henry V (r. 1414–22), an event widely celebrated as a restoration of original English dominions. The monk-historian Thomas Walsingham, for instance, wrote a large chronicle, the *Hypodigma Neustriae*, or 'Paradigm of Normandy', structuring English history on the principle that the pattern of English conquest had finally reached its fulfillment. The victory was followed by an agreement in 1420 that France would give the English king and his heirs the crown of France as well as England.

Henry V died before this could be fulfilled in himself, and his unimpressive son Henry VI (r. 1422–61, with interruptions) was crowned king of France in 1430 in a crushingly expensive and unpopular ceremony. This particularly feckless king was subsequently persuaded to give away both Normandy and France as part of an arranged marriage with Margaret of Anjou, in 1445. The marriage admirably served the purposes of the French king Charles VII, but it seems not to have served any English purposes at all. Perhaps not even Henry's: he was absent from the wedding, sending the Earl of Suffolk as his proxy.

Political chaos, driven by the aspirants to the throne by the descendants of Edward III's third son, Edmund of Langley, Duke of York, followed the losses of Normandy and France on a scale not seen since the 'Anarchy' of Stephen's reign, and capped by the final insanity of Henry VI. At this point, the throne passed first to the great-grandson of Edmund of Langley, Edward IV (r. 1461–83), then, after his death, to his son, Edward V, almost at once killed by his uncle, Richard Duke of Gloucester, who thus gained the throne himself (r. 1483–5). This state of virtual civil war was settled only by the abrupt intrusion and the very different style of the originally Welsh Tudors, distant relatives, through marriage and female descendants, of the Lancastrian line: Henry VII (r. 1485–1509) and, especially, his son Henry VIII (r. 1509–53). These, fortunately, had few family members to compete for the throne, and they possessed a style of royal autocracy that for once was welcome.

Henry VI's catastrophically incompetent reign, and the rival power struggles that followed it and destroyed forever the prospect of a united England and France, may be seen as the real end of 'medieval England', disintegrating into a blur of civil war around a king who was feeble-witted or clinically depressed, or simply profoundly incapable of any political calculation. The final confrontation between King Henry VIII and the Roman (and English) church seems part of a new 'age' beyond the 'middle' one. Yet that conflict began, as had Henry II's with Becket, with the traditional medieval question of the legal immunity of criminal clerics. Only later did the more explosive question of Henry's ability to divorce Catherine of Aragon emerge. Henry VIII not only prevailed over 'his' archbishops on these claims against the pope, he was also able to crush papal authority in England in a legal sense altogether, marshaling parliament to help him take possession of the kingdom's monasteries, first the smaller then the greater ones, on the grounds of reforming a corrupt and immoral church as well as removing an inconvenient subservience to Rome.

Henry VIII's gesture was by then fully 'Christian' because of the new kinds of Continental theology that could bolster such 'Reformist' actions at the end of the long dance, or duel, of medieval clergy and kingship. As intellectual supporter, Henry VIII had the Reformist preacher and scholar William Tyndale. The latter's translations of the Bible, and his caustic sermons against the Roman church, provided Henry with an important basis for any royal supremacy over the church. 'This book is for me and all kings to read,' Henry is said to have declared when he read Tyndale's lambasting of the clergy, *The Practyse of Prelates* (Constant 1966: 16).

THE CLERGY AND THE INTELLECTUAL WORLD

This history of kings and high politics has often involved the 'second' estate of England, the clergy. More generally, most medieval intellectual, cultural and literary production must be understood somewhat in terms of the clerical world and its influence. By the later Middle Ages, perhaps one in fifty of the population was a cleric of some kind (Swanson 1989: 30–6) but their influence was much larger than this suggests. All the topics that fall under a history of the medieval clerical world reach into the non-clerical world: sooner or later, nearly every 'clerical' issue becomes a 'lay' one.

The religious orders

The world of institutional religion in medieval England was enormously diverse. Priests, who regularly consecrated the Eucharist and guided the laity from birth to death, are a constant feature of the medieval religious world from the establishment of the parish system sometime in the tenth century. As members of the 'secular' clergy (i.e. living 'among the world'), they were part of a group including deacons, archdeacons, bishops and archbishops, all of whom, like the priests, occupied particular territories – parishes or sees – over whose souls they took charge.

These clergy were surrounded by other religious groups that rose and fell in dominance. From the seventh century until the Dissolution in 1537, monasteries were the heart of the church's economic and intellectual powers, maintained by the properties, prayers and studies of monks and nuns living under an abbot and in accord with the Rule of St Benedict, dwelling apart from the world of the laity. Here, unlike many other domains in medieval culture, women might gain a powerful position, especially in early medieval centuries when an abbess like Hild of Whitby, of Bede's period, might rule over both monks and nuns in a 'double-monastery'. Late medieval nunneries, however, were consistently under-endowed compared to late medieval monasteries, and the standards of learning for women religious neither expected nor encouraged them to attain Latin fluency or engage in the kinds of writing that male monks might produce. The learned and highly productive women who overcame these circumstances were giants of intellect and determination indeed.

By the later twelfth century, a new kind of social mobility for men at least emerged that depended on the intellect and led to new forms of clerical life. Rather than remain in a monastery as a monk's vows of 'stability' required, the dynamic and forensic clerics and debaters appearing from the mid-twelfth century on, like Abelard, John of Salisbury, Peter Lombard and many others, moved between serving important functions in lords' or kings' or popes' courts to teaching groups of passionate clerical disciples around them, first at cathedral schools (which replaced monasteries as the centers of intellectual training) then at the universities emerging at Oxford, Paris, Bologna and then Cambridge. Soon other religious orders appeared that were often centered in cities and mingled freely among the secular world. Stirred by a desire to follow the true 'apostolic life', by wandering and begging as the apostles of Jesus had, St Francis, in Assisi, Italy, threw away the money, and the clothing, of his successful bourgeois family to found the ultimately very widespread and massively influential order of the Franciscan friars. With their renunciation (in theory) of property and life in the world, so different from the ancient tradition of the monastic life, they were as much a part of the new urban social mobility as the increases in trade, urbanization and record-keeping. St Dominic, founder of the Dominicans or 'preaching order', followed soon after Francis, establishing an order that particularly dominated the universities just beginning to emerge.

The plethora of new religious ways of life in the twelfth and thirteenth centuries challenged the supremacy of the monastic tradition, in which a vastly wealthy institution held monks in a secure place to serve the world by praying for the souls of those in the world (especially their secular founders and benefactors). Monasteries continued to be the centers of historical writing, and certainly to be the largest institutional landlords (thus they were special targets of the rebellious peasants in 1381). Some late-medieval monasteries had important intellectuals and writers, such as Ranulph Higden (d. 1365), Thomas Walsingham (d. 1422), and the English poet John Lydgate (d. 1449). But their religious calling became only one of an array of options for spiritual and intellectual vocation.

Indeed, beyond all these official orders was an expanding group of at least somewhat educated clergy who were not lucky enough to find any official position as religious professionals, or who chose to marry, which after the eleventh-century reforms denied them ordination as priests. The numbers of such unbeneficed clerics seem increasingly large in the fourteenth and fifteenth centuries, when many found employment in odd-job spiritual work, such as singing for the souls of a chantry's dead founder and perhaps his family (although, as Geoffrey Chaucer's Parson and William Langland's Prologue from the late fourteenth century both remind us, even a beneficed priest might want to abandon his parish and head to London 'To seken hym a chaunterie for soules': Chaucer, *General Prologue* 510; *Piers Plowman* B. Prologue 83–6). The jobs for 'chantry priests' grew increasingly common in the fourteenth and fifteenth centuries, as the view of Purgatory became clearer and seemingly more negotiable, making both the laity's uses of clergy easier to define and perhaps the clergy's status less august than in earlier medieval centuries. Such unbeneficed clergy's differences from at least some of the laity could, by the later fourteenth century, seem remarkably small. The poet Thomas Hoccleve, trained as a priest but finally employed in the king's Privy Seal office, records how he 'waytid faste [*watched eagerly*] / Aftir sum benefice, and whan noon cam, / Be procees [*In the course of time*] I me weddid ate laste' (*Regiment of Princes*, lines 1451–3). On the other side, simply being literate (in the sense of knowing how to read Latin) associated one with clerical status. Gower, a lawyer, very learned but certainly not a priest, refers to himself as a 'burel [i.e. unlearned, i.e. unclerical] clerk' (*Confessio Amantis*, Prol. 52). Chaucer's Reeve is adept enough at account-keeping to conceal his embezzling, and with Chaucer's description of his haircut almost a tonsure ('dokked lyk a preest') and his cloak like a friar's ('Tukked . . . as is a frere aboute'), the Reeve seems to exists, like many, in a nether category between laity and clergy (*General Prologue*, lines 590, 621).

Literacy and book-making

In part this late medieval blurring between lay and clerical status was due to increasing literacy. It is certainly naive to say that knowledge simply *is* power; but knowledge has at least a kind of power, one shaped and charged by how exclusively such knowledge is held by some particular group, and with what importance for the well-being of everyone else. The clergy's contributions to and control over literate culture is far more profound in England than most other European countries; the clergy's importance in England from the earliest period had the enormous benefit of having conferred vernacular literacy onto the culture far earlier and more widely than elsewhere, but the clergy's tenacious hold later on intellectual culture in England may also explain the lag in secular literary culture and a non-clerical intelligentsia compared, for instance, to Italy's mercantile and aristocratic culture. Certainly, forms of secular intellectual culture flourished in England from the twelfth century on; by the later thirteenth century, it was not ridiculous to call a knight *litteratus*; and by the early fifteenth century at least half the merchants in London were 'literate' in the sense of using and producing documents of many kinds, including theological pamphlets and personal letters. But clerical intellectual culture remained dominant, and did so even up to the Reformation, which was fed if not instigated by 'reformist' clerical thought.

The history of medieval book-making tracks this development and, like it, remains tied to the history of the clergy. Medieval books were hand-copied codices, using vegetable dye as ink, and made first from treated animal skins, then, by the later fourteenth century, increasingly often paper. Until the twelfth century, books were made almost exclusively in monasteries; they were large, often elaborate and rare, their scripts ornate and their visual designs – especially in the magnificent Latin Bibles from Northumbria and Ireland – sometimes dizzyingly intricate, a matter for long meditation rather than efficient use. By the twelfth century, book-makers are found in a range of urban and royal settings as well as religious houses, and the kinds of informal scripts used in charters, designed for faster writing than book-hand, began to be transferred to books themselves. By the thirteenth century, cursive handwriting was standard in books, as were increasingly terse abbreviations, especially for Latin: a medieval academic text, perhaps the most densely efficient kind of text of all medieval texts because so many had to be produced, is difficult now for even a specialist to decipher. The academic world also contributed the 'pecia' or 'piece' system, using several scribes at once to copy a book's different sections (quires). By the later fourteenth century, professional scribes were common and even had a guild in London, although their operations were ad hoc, not yet organized into fixed establishments for book-making of English works. By the fifteenth century, the English book trade was an organized activity in cities, producing English books either on consignment or in ready-made sections that buyers would request to be assembled according to their wishes. By mid-century the 'paper revolution' had arrived, allowing much cheaper manuscripts; by the late fifteenth century, the printing press was established in England, carrying considerably further the process of spreading learning beyond the exclusive control of the clergy.

Books for clerics were usually in Latin, and thus Latin books predominate in medieval culture, although they do not dominate in the modern classes devoted to medieval writing. Particularly popular works include Boethius's late fifth-century *De Consolatione Philosophiae*, well known through the fifteenth century; Jacob of Voragine's *Legenda Aurea*, a collection of saints' lives from the 1280s which survives in over a thousand copies; Geoffrey of Monmouth's Arthurian *History of the Kings of Britain*, in hundreds of copies; and of course the Latin Bible, which survives in many more. These are only a few notable examples. Copies of French books were much less numerous, but could sometimes be significant: the *Roman de la Rose* (1235–75), the most popular vernacular work of literature of the Middle Ages and well known in England, is preserved in over 300 copies. Works in English were still less widely copied. Single copies of major works are not uncommon from *Beowulf* (copied at the turn of the eleventh century) to *Sir Gawain and the Green Knight* (copied at the turn of the fifteenth).

As one reaches the fifteenth century, however, increasing copying of English works is as evident as that of works in Latin and French. Whereas from the Anglo-Saxon period only single copies of nearly every English text have come down to us, English works from late medieval England are sometimes preserved in dozens or more. The confessor's guide and handbook of moral theology in English, *The Pricke of Conscience*, written in the mid-fourteenth century, exists in 115 fifteenth-century copies. More elite literary artifacts are represented more sparsely but still in substantially more copies than English works in any earlier periods. *The Canterbury Tales* exists (in whole or part) in 82 copies; *Piers Plowman* and Gower's *Confessio Amantis* both exist in dozens of copies; the virulently anti-Semitic, alliterative *Siege of Jerusalem* exists in nine. Nearly all copies of these late fourteenth-century works are from after 1417, when Henry V began using English in all his correspondence. The English translation of the Bible that John Wyclif's followers produced in the late fourteenth century is found in some 250 copies from the fifteenth century, owned by nobility as well as merchants. Although Wyclif's heresy was condemned on all sides, the accurate English translation of the Bible that his followers produced was immensely useful to a laity with greater capacities for reading and great interest in the religious materials that in earlier centuries had been conveyed to them only through priests. King Henry VI donated his personal copy (now Bodleian Library, MS Bodley 277) to the London Carthusians.

Lay and religious women increasingly often appear as writers as well as book-owners, readers and patrons in the later fourteenth and fifteenth century, often but not always with male clerical guidance. Women were the main protectors and disciples of the mystical writer Richard Rolle (d. 1349), and a high proportion of English religious writing through the mid-fourteenth century was produced for women. Aristocratic women were especially the intended readership for the elegant books of hours that proliferate in late medieval culture, often with stunningly beautiful pictures accompanying the liturgical texts. It has been argued that a major engine driving increases in literacy was women's reading of such devotional texts (Clanchy [1993], pp. 189–96). Women of course need not have limited their reading to that. A copy of *Piers Plowman* was granted in the will of a London rector to one Agnes Eggesfield in 1396, one of the earliest named owners of that poem (R. A. Wood, 'A fourteenth-century London owner of *Piers Plowman*', *Medium Ævum* 53 (1984): 83–90). A mid-fifteenth century treatise on carnal and spiritual love written for a nun quotes repeatedly and perceptively from Chaucer's *Troilus and Criseyde* (see Patterson [1987], pp. 114–53). Over a hundred letters were composed by the women in the East Anglian Paston family through the fifteenth century. But except for a few shaky signatures all of those were dictated to male clerks or family members.

Dogma and theology

If the clergy were pervasive as writers and teachers, they also promoted the cohesion and circulation of many ideas and even many stories, in their constant efforts to teach and guide the laity at all social levels. Teaching the Creed and the Pater Noster was a basic step; teaching the laity to scrutinize themselves in terms of sin and error was fundamental as well. After the Fourth Lateran Council of 1215, and still more with further clerical efforts in England to publicize doctrine to the laity from the Council of Lambeth in 1280 on, confession was an annual obligation for all the laity over twelve years old. This explains the vast array of writings from the early fourteenth century in Latin, French and English that offer guidance on vices and virtues, often representing them in intriguing narratives as well as more direct explanation, written for priests to supply them with the means to carry out their role.

Penance itself became more textual. In the early Middle Ages, penance for sins often involved public acts of self-punishment or other ritual displays, ranging from wearing a white gown on the church doorstep in Anglo-Saxon England to making barefoot pilgrimages, as Henry II was forced to do after the murder of Thomas Becket. In the later Middle Ages, penance more often involved paying specified fines. This 'spiritual economy' based on investments into and withdrawals from the 'treasury of grace' might be seen in contractual terms even by medieval clerics. From the thirteenth century, the idea was officially entrenched that purgatory was a specified punitive zone leading ultimately to paradise. By that point, the idea of purchasing an 'indulgence' for sin, an officially sealed document, often shifted from its orthodox sense, as a mere remission of the earthly punishment of one's sin, to a more vulgar, contractual notion of paying and praying one's own or a deceased other's way to a shorter period in purgatory. This led to a whole industry of pardoners and chantries, the latter private chapels staffed by priests who were given an endowment to pray a certain number of times to alleviate the punishments of a deceased patron's sins.

Clerical writings (including some English ones, such as *Dives and Pauper* [1405–10]) displayed much effort in subtlety resisting this vulgar notion of 'purchasing paradise', and late medieval literature not only satirized but also more subtly probed this view. The naive, grieving narrator in the fourteenth-century poem *Pearl* believes that spiritual rewards must always be earned directly through the direct merit of good works through a long life, until the scholastically informed soul of his two-year old daughter informs him that God's grace is needed to make any works, however seemingly good, and any life, however long, worthy of spiritual rewards. Surely many other people must have thought as the bereaved narrator did, though some may have been similarly corrected, albeit by more earthly teachers.

The full range of medieval theology was in fact not a matter only of penitential reflection or unthinking obedience to dogma and authority. Rather, it was a vigorous and subtle intellectual pursuit, whose focus was doctrinal conviction, faith and mystical experience, but whose results reached far from those matters into a wide and subtle range of philosophy and psychology, including theory about time, mathematics and language.

This range is clear even in the earliest period, when the rejection of 'pagan' philosophy and culture in favor of Christian faith was strongest. The early church Fathers – Tertullian, Jerome (translator of the Hebrew and Greek Bible into Latin), Ambrose, Gregory the Great and, above all, Augustine – established a very large repository of models and materials that centuries of clerical culture throughout western Christian culture rehearsed, pondered and re-applied. These writers offered vigorous polemics, overarching reinterpretations of history into Christian terms and psychologically acute analyzes of the soul, nearly all with an essentially Platonic assumption (carried over from the New Testament itself) that higher realities radiated through the material particulars of human and natural existence, and that the clerical vocation provided a life dedicated to following that higher love.

Thus for Augustine (d. 430), the most elegantly cogent and influential of all the fathers, the progress of history is a struggle between two groups of peoples, or 'cities', obedient to two kinds of love. *Cupiditas* is a desire focused on 'enjoying' (*fruor*) the world directly, seeking in it the full presence that only God supplies; *caritas* is a love of the world only insofar as one can 'use' it (*utor*) as a means to the one thing that can be fully 'enjoyed', God (*De doctrina Christiana* [427], bk. 1; and *De civitate Dei* [425], especially bk. 13). So too, Augustine's *De trinitate* (*c.* 414) deftly assesses the human soul's integrated yet discrete capacities of memory, will and understanding – and even the extraordinary human capacity to conceive a thought as an inner word: these are explored as analogies to the unity yet discrete and dynamic properties of the Trinity, and small versions of how the divine Word was made flesh (e.g. John 1).

Theology and sacred history like this offered a powerful approach to what we might call psychology, and in varying ways it contributed to an array of English medieval literature, from *The Seafarer* (? eighth century), through Chaucer's *Troilus and Criseyde* (*c.* 1386), and beyond. This outlook implied an essential sense of faith in Platonic higher realities and, in turn, as it was readily sustained in the seventh through eleventh centuries in the monasteries (the centers of learning in England as elsewhere in that period), it became correlated to the monastic principle of obedience to authority. Beginning in the mid-twelfth century, however, as intellectual activity began to shift to cathedral schools such as Chartres and Orléans, then universities such as Oxford and Paris, an interest in exploring pagan writers in their own terms appears. More significantly, so does an interest in exploring Christian thought itself by means of the materials of and strategies for inquiry in Aristotle's writings, which began rapidly to gain attention. Some of Aristotle's writings were already available in Latin from Boethius's sixth-century translations (the 'Categories' and 'On Interpretation'); in the mid-twelfth century many other Latin translations from Greek were freshly made and, rather miraculously, a host of lost translations of Aristotle by Boethius were suddenly discovered.

Aristotle was not a source of more authority but of powerful new tools for reasoning. The new interest in sifting and questioning evidence, and applying rational inquiry and organization to all topics, fit well into a new range of career options for intellectuals. Their capabilities were needed as much for public roles in serving kings in the state-building and law-building that emerged in Western Europe in the period, as for the private tutoring of the children of the nobility, including the young women who could not learn Latin with the men in the cathedral schools but who nonetheless occasionally received excellent private instruction (as Abelard privately tutored Heloise, until he fell in love with and secretly married her, whereupon her uncle castrated him and sent her to a monastery).

Thanks to the universities, more adventurous topics such as the legitimacy of different religious orders and the definition of the true 'apostolic life' (as we might say, How would Jesus's disciples live?) were aired in increasingly more public domains. The fierce arguments between some of the religious orders over these questions fueled a range of literary satire in Latin, French, then English, and reached a wider world in public sermons. During the fourteenth and fifteenth centuries, such criticism shifted from being satire of one order against another to satire against *all* clerical orders. These critiques were amplified by the rise of Lollardy in the late fourteenth century.

This movement began when John Wyclif (d. 1384), master of Baliol College until 1361, advanced the theory, derived from the Austin Friars, that 'dominion' (ownership and control of property) should belong to those who have divine grace, and that when Emperor Constantine had endowed the church with its temporal wealth the church began to become corrupt. The present, institutional church, therefore, should be dispossessed of its property. Moreover, since only God could discern the most perfect individual, only he knew the true pope. A much more dangerous claim was that the Eucharist after consecration did not stop being material bread and wine, although it became infused with the 'substance' of Christ's body and blood. More, the worship before the images of the saints was blasphemous because it implied worship of the images themselves – a view that fore-shadowed the widespread destructions of sacred statues in the Reformation.

Wyclif, who was publicly condemned at the London 'Earthquake' council of 1382 (when a tremor seemed to confirm the judgement), gained a strong and well-endowed group of followers who wrote considerable quantities of polemical theology, sermons and commentaries in English and made a full translation of the Bible, all of which they dis-seminated in numerous, carefully regular copies. Indeed, the central-midlands dialect of English cultivated by the Lollards has a claim to be an earlier 'standard English' before King Henry V from a more orthodox position established his own (see Blake 1996: 169–70).

The Lollards failed to achieve anything beyond what Anne Hudson calls a 'premature reformation', perhaps because the intellectual subtlety of some of their views limited the move-ment's following. Certainly the printing press, and John Tyndale's access to the king's ear, helped the Puritans where the Lollards failed. Lollardy, however, succeeded in holding tenacious groups of followers throughout the fifteenth century, some in rural communities, some in cities like Leicester and a few among the aristocracy. Sir John Oldcastle was burned for heresy in 1417, roundly condemned for his insubordinate desire to think as a clerk might in the 'Compleint to Sir John Oldcastle' by the lapsed clerk Thomas Hoccleve.

THOSE WHO WORKED

The great majority of the population throughout the whole span was composed of those who produced the fruits of the earth or of livestock in one way or another and under the shadow of one or another kind of landlord. Some of these labored for themselves as free peasants and perhaps as managers of other laborers, but many labored for landlords as servile laborers (serfs, villeins or 'customary tenants'). Others, increasingly from the thirteenth century on, labored for other property holders as hired laborers, as part of the growth of a monetary culture.

The agrarian base of medieval English life was far wider and more important than many of us in the early twenty-first century in the West are able easily to comprehend. It is certainly suggested by the use of metaphors in preaching and poetry about the 'ploughshare of the tongue' or the ox-team of the pen (Chaucer, *Knight's Tale*, 886–7), or of the interpretation of texts as 'cultivating the vineyard of the text'. Yet few medieval writers focused on this mass of people in their most regular activities, except in times of famine, social disorder or rebellion. In his eleventh-century *Colloquy* to teach schoolboys Latin, Ælfric presents a ploughman ('yrþlingc') describing his hard labors, assisted by a boy; some of the English lyrics in the early fourteenth-century manuscript in the British Library known as Harley MS 2253 seem sympathetic to the harassment of the poor by minor officials, but in terms that may also be interpreted as satirizing the poor themselves; the monk Thomas Walsingham describes the rebellion of 1381 at St Albans with particularly caustic satire of the pathetic 'rustics' in his Latin *Deeds of the Abbots*.

Even these are unusual moments of glimpsing this mass of people, and they are distorted or oblique views. Still more is the gruesome, troll-like peasant shepherd (or rather, wild-beast-herd) near the beginning of Chrétien de Troyes' twelfth-century *Yvain*, whose most shocking statement is to declare to an amazed knight, 'Je sui uns hon' ('I am a man', line 330). The idealized plowman in the late fourteenth-century *Piers Plowman*, a near-allegory of virtue and faithful labor for his lord, St Truth, is a rare, perhaps unique image. Chaucer casually ridicules the impoverished dairymaid who owns an exuberantly courtly rooster in *The Nun's Priest's Tale*; her dull virtues and good health derive chiefly from how little she can afford to eat: 'Repleccioun ne made hire nevere sik' (2837). Gower turns them into hideous and pathetic chimeras, pigs with elephant tusks and flies with dogs' teeth, when describing the rebellion of 1381 in his Latin *Vox clamantis*.

To summarize 80 per cent of the population at a stroke would risk similarly reductive caricatures. But we may say in a general way that peasants carried out hard physical work and lived in humble 'vills', that is, sets of houses often near a village church and, usually, near a single manor house belonging to the owner of the local property and perhaps of many other manor houses like it. This might be either a secular lord, who would likely endeavor to keep the property in the family or add to it by strategic marriages, or a religious institution. Either the secular or the ecclesiastical landlord would likely also 'own' a given amount of the labor of the peasants who lived on the land with 'customary' duties attached, and who were his, or its, villeins, whose labor was in effect part of the property's value. They were responsible for working the nearby two or (after the thirteenth century) three open fields, which in rotation would lie fallow and which were often cooperatively ploughed (in precise arrangements of shared labor) using equipment that was similarly owned in common.

This land was divided into *carrucates* – stretches that would take a day's work with the heavy plough (*carruca*) favored in England from the Anglo-Saxon period on. M. Postan suggests that little changed in the technology of agrarian production for so long because the chief uses of the surplus money gained from it went not back into agrarian production itself, but into other needs felt more keenly by knights or monks intent on upholding the demands of their own 'status'. A knight would use his profits from the land to expand his retinues and other prestige-gaining elements of knightly endeavor. A monastery would invest its profits in church building and book-making. A laborer had neither the social power nor the legal status to demand that the profits of his work be used to improve his mode of production.

Along with various forms of customary tenancy (possession of a property carrying the obligation to perform certain tasks), slavery was known in early Anglo-Saxon England, but it waned by the tenth century and was abolished by the twelfth. Probably a holdover from Roman culture, slavery may also have developed from the conquests of the native Celts by the invading Saxons from the late fifth century on. The Anglo-Saxon word *wealh* can mean 'foreigner', 'stranger', 'slave' or 'Welshman'; the word *ðeow* means both 'slave' and 'servant'; these two words together are probably indicated in the name of King Hrothgar's politic wife in *Beowulf*, Wealhtheow.

The legal status of serfdom, which throve as outright slavery waned, was onerous enough, although it was chiefly an economic burden. Serfs, or villeins, and their family members were formally required to pay a fine when selling property or moving away, at the death of a head of household, at the marriage of a daughter or even (for bondswomen only) upon having unmarried sexual intercourse; the terms of such fees were highly specified and carried significant economic and social burdens: 'heriot' for the giving of the 'best beast' as a death-tax; 'merchet' for the marriage fee; 'leyr-wite' for a bondswoman's fornication.

The numbers and opportunities of serfs ebbed and flowed in post-Conquest England, punctuated by a few moments of crisis. The mid-twelfth century was politically unsettled under the civil war between Stephen and Matilda, so lords tended to give up on managing far-distant manors and vills and rent them out instead. This circumstance seems to have encouraged villeins to purchase or be given manumission (freedom from villein status). But in the thirteenth century customary tenancy gained back some dominance when landlords expanded territories through reclamation of marshland and forests, keeping much of that, and thus their workers, under their direct management (as 'demesne' land). In the thirteenth century even communities that had formerly been free were claimed by landlords (including the church) to have servile status. Thus began a long struggle between customary tenants and landlords that developed through a series of local conflicts in the fourteenth century, culminating with the largest and most coordinated uprising England had ever seen, in mid-June 1381.

This began in Kent and Suffolk, where traditions of agrarian freedom were strongest; thus perhaps it began where offenses seemed all the less tolerable, in the light of the much-depressed population levels of laborers in this period, which allowed them to demand significantly greater wages than before (and, in spite of legislation in 1351 against such demands, the scarcity of labor after the Black Death drove wages steadily up). Another period of rebellions began in 1450, fostered by Jack Cade; these ended with less violent repressions, but were part of a period of generally volatile conflict between the major factions of Lancaster and York that emerged during the minority, and built up during the insanity or incompetence, of Henry VI.

Serfdom disappeared gradually in the fifteenth century, not because of any revolutionary demands but because of a general shift toward manumissions as a way for lords to raise incomes, along with lords' increasing emphasis on renting rather than directly managing far-flung properties. Heirs of villeins often entered into their parents' lands under the more precise, documented terms of 'copyhold', which typically stipulated money rent with no 'customary' labors attached. Substantial freemen also took over lands formerly owned by villeins, similarly extinguishing the lands' traditions of customary duties. Common law began to protect the tenure of copyhold, now that this was being used by anyone who could pay for it. By the reign of Elizabeth, peasant labor, from field work to sheep farming, still supported most economic production, but manufacturing, trade and exploration began to occupy a greater proportion of economic activity, recovering from a slump of nearly a century as the population recovered and as precious metals began to be available in much greater quantities. Amid these changes villeinage and the legal category of the 'unfree' vanished, dissolved into the greater anonymity and alienation of a more contractual, mercantile culture.

2

Medieval English Literature: Genres, Canons and Literary Communities

---

When we step into the world of medieval English writing, we must orient ourselves not only to a set of linguistic, religious, cultural and political circumstances and assumptions, but also to the kinds of literary forms and traditions that are valued, suppressed or transformed in any given instance. The 'original author' is not exclusively responsible for the literary forms we encounter; these are also the results of the context of readers, institutions and patrons who requested or preserved or gathered the works that we open up, as well as of the traditions that established the modes as well as a vast repository of stories. Narratives often emerge and circulate in a way that makes it seem that the stories came first, and any particular author only later. Moreover, in an age when all books were hand-written, no copy is made like any other or undergoes a history of use and reshaping like any other.

The same work can appear in very different settings, often implying different kinds of emphasis or indeed of genre – as, for instance, religious instruction or historical information or less purposefully defined entertainment.

This is not to deny that the crafting and re-crafting, combining or expanding, of narrative materials, styles and forms can be brilliantly and imaginatively original, or that individual writers or groups of writers can mark major shifts in literary developments. But if genre can be defined as the focus, subject and form of a work, in medieval writing it offers a busy and mobile meeting point between past traditions that are re-created, combined or suppressed within a particular work, and subsequent selection and remaking after it has been 'finished' (if it is not, indeed, further continued, another common mode of medieval literary and other narrative production).

To try to keep these issues in view while surveying medieval English writing, we can take two tacks. We can start by tracing historically the genres and clusters of writers that emerged and were fostered in each period, using the political and cultural 'period' designations identified in the previous chapter: Anglo-Saxon England, from the seventh century to the Norman Conquest in 1066; Anglo-Norman England, from the Conquest through the twelfth century or a bit beyond; and later medieval England, from the thirteenth through the fifteenth centuries. The second tack will be to take up in somewhat more formal focus and detail the genres that appear throughout this span, although in changing forms. This tack will use the categories of literary genre to frame history, rather than the reverse.

HISTORICAL OVERVIEW

Anglo-Saxon literary communities and literary canons

To trace the cluster of English writers from Anglo-Saxon England, we must start with the moment when most of them were preserved in the form that has been passed down to us, although that is late in the period. A substantial majority of the 'classical' English poetry we possess from this period – some 30,000 lines in all – is copied in just four medieval books, which we call the Exeter book, the Vercelli book, the Junius Manuscript and the *Beowulf* Manuscript (the names are entirely modern, as are the titles of all the poems and, indeed, of nearly all medieval poems). These were put together around the year 1000, probably in major monasteries such as Winchester and Exeter (where the largest of these books remained), and all were written in essentially a common poetic form of West Saxon dialect. These preserve the only surviving copies of nearly all the poems. Only 'Body and Soul', a short debate between a corpse and its eternal soul, appears in two of these (Exeter and Junius); a short lyrical section is shared by *Daniel* and *Azarias*, in Junius and Exeter respectively. Moreover, the Cross's speech in *Dream of the Rood* partly appears inscribed on two crosses, of which – the earliest and grandest, the stone Ruthwell Cross – is dated *c*.730. A number of other poems appear amid the prose entries of the *Anglo-Saxon Chronicle*, whose five surviving copies date from the tenth and eleventh centuries. A few poems are known from single scraps or, in the case of *The Battle of Maldon*, as a seventeenth-century copy of a fragment that was then burned in the Cotton library fire of 1731, but it had already been heavily damaged before being copied.

Just as the language is generally consistent, so the poetic style is consistent as well, at least in some smaller units: beyond the few direct repetitions noted, phrases and even scenic styles are occasionally repeated or slightly varied. Yet such poetry is remarkable for the exquisite variety and richness of literary effect it generates from a relatively narrow range of linguistic and stylistic options. The *Beowulf* poet's inclusion of other stories in the 'digressions', providing background or possible thematic parallels to the events taking place, is just one original way to develop formal and thus thematic richness within the relatively severe poetic constraints of Anglo-Saxon English poetry.

Dating the 'original' works, except for the poems about recent historical events, is therefore very difficult, all the more so since the poetry seems to value poetic traditions and visions of 'olden days'. We have a single early eleventh-century copy of *Beowulf*, but its materials and style allow it to be placed as early as the eight century or as late as the manuscript itself (see Chase 1997). Much of the poetry probably was produced before West Saxon dominance, which absorbed and effaced almost all previous English writing. The eighth-century Ruthwell Cross in Cumberland, now south-west Scotland, in which parts of the *Dream of the Rood* were inscribed, was in Northumbrian territory; signs of Mercian origins are clear in a number of entries in the *Anglo-Saxon Chronicle*, as in some of the homilies collected in the 'Vercelli' book; a poet named Cynewulf signed his name in runes at the end of a number of poems that show traces of an Anglian dialect and thus are likely to be from the ninth century when Mercian culture was at its height. The ninth-century Anglian origins of *Beowulf* have also been argued.

Certainly some editing and selection occurred in West Saxon religious houses, but earlier kinds of selection had already occurred. Nearly all of this poetry is essentially Christian, most of it overtly so. In the case of *Beowulf*, although it condemns pagan worship, the poem offers a eulogizing look back on a pagan aristocratic but somewhat dispossessed hero, who navigates an extraordinarily detailed and vivid world of Germanic, supposedly pagan culture to rise to high power and great renown, and to test the limits of how righteous and admirable a pre-Christian hero can be. This, like other elements in the poetry, suggests a strong tradition of native poetry that preceded and probably surrounded Christian influence.

Some sense that the Christian poems that have been so carefully collected and preserved were likely not the only kinds of poems known in Anglo-Saxon England can be glimpsed from the famous scene told by Bede (in 731) about an illiterate swineherd at a monastery, Cædmon, from *c*.680. This swineherd slipped away from a mead-hall celebration as the harp and the turn to recite approached him, because he did not know any songs to contribute. Falling asleep in his stable, he was instructed in a dream-vision by an angel about how to make a new kind of Christian song in English. After telling his reeve, he was taken to the abbess and her senior monks, who at once made him a monk and gave him the regular task of transforming Latin Scriptural stories into 'the most melodious verse' in 'English, his own tongue'. Henceforth he spent his his days being read Latin Scripture then processing it, 'like some clean animal chewing the cud', and turning it into piously mellifluous English poetry (*Ecclesiastical History* 4.24).

Bede recorded Cædmon's divinely inspired first poem only in Latin, but the earliest manuscripts of Bede's works (from *c*.800 Northumbria) have an English version written above the Latin prose, and this is among the earliest datable English poetry (the lines on the Ruthwell Cross are probably slightly earlier). The Northumbrian English ends, 'eci Dryctin æfter tiadæ / firum foldu, Frea allmehtig' ('the eternal Lord afterwards made the earth for men, the Lord almighty'). Frea was a Norse god, but the phrase is absorbed as a mere synonym for the Christian God (as it is used in longer and presumably much later Christian poetry as well, such as *Genesis*, 'frea ælmihtig', line 5). Christian poetic exploitation of Germanic traditions here seems already natural.

Whatever songs were being sung at Cædmon's feast-hall, there seems little hope of finding some direct source of 'pagan poetry' in the written English verse from Anglo-Saxon England. Some possibilities, most in other Germanic languages, are suggested below under 'Epic and historical poetry: Anglo-Saxon England' in the survey of genres. Certainly Christian biblical language is fluently absorbed into the texture of even the most heroic Anglo-Saxon poetry: in *Beowulf*, Beowulf is said to descend into the deep pool to fight Grendel's mother at *nones*, a Latin word for the ninth hour of the day, as when Jesus died (Luke 23:44). Indeed, it is useful to stress that the dominant tradition, or literary 'movement', of Christian English poems invokes pagan styles and even pagan heroes but do so to revitalize a range of basically Christian issues: the importance of free choice for good or ill; the divine, if sometimes mysterious, meaning of history; the tawdriness of worldly goals; the power of faith and loyalty to a divine or human ruler. None of the English poetry of Anglo-Saxon England simply proclaims what a Latin (or English) sermon might on these topics; yet its narratives provoke intriguing questions about all of those topics. How do the ethics in the aristocratic, pagan world of *Beowulf* measure up to Christian ones, and what are the implications for the divine meaning of history? Should Beowulf have risked, and lost, his life in such a daring way, since he was a king with a people who depended on him? Since loyalty to a divine lord is crucial, does the Cross's warrior-like loyalty to Jesus in *The Dream of the Rood* extend to 'holding firm' as the very means of Jesus's crucifixion? And is it better for warriors themselves to die on the same principle, in *The Battle of Maldon*, after their lord proudly allows fair battle-position to the 'slaughter-wolves', the Vikings, and himself is sacrificed for his ideals?

These provocations of ethical, social and historical questions are signs of an intellectually vital context of Christian writers and readers, and aristocratic or royally connected ones, as all the major West Saxon monasteries were where the poetry was recorded. A similar context explains the magisterial *Anglo-Saxon Chronicle*, which offers dense, annalistic accounts of kings, nobles and major national events, produced in five different monasteries in a concerted proclamation of West Saxon unity and authority, a posture also clear from the translations of major Christian writings sponsored by King Alfred (see below under genres: 'Prose: Anglo-Saxon England').

In the later stages of Anglo-Saxon England appear prose works addressing a much wider audience. Two major prose homilists, Ælfric (*c.*1000) and Wulfstan (*c.*1015), open up the range of written literary options by maintaining a fluent, accessible, vigorous, yet often deftly rhythmical and repetitive prose. Their writings offer basic dogma and saints' lives, social criticism and moral exhortation. They also include some discussion of pagan practices that derive from Norse influences, including comments on the cults of Odin, Thor and Freya (or Frigg), the 'shameless goddess' (in Ælfric's treatise *De falsis deis*, which Wulfstan rewrote). Possibly that new attention to 'real' paganism was responding to influences from the Danes who by then occupied nearly half of England, the Danelaw (although they had agreed to Christian conversion as part of the Treaty of Wedmore, 878). Attention to unorthodoxy may also have been because of the wider social world on which these preachers necessarily focused, and where orthodox Christian learning cannot be assumed as it can in the monastic poetry. A collection of recipes and spells from the eleventh century provides a glimpse of that more 'popular' world: it includes spells to cure horses that have been 'elf-shot', chants to the 'mother of earth' to cure plots of earth that sorcerers have poisoned, and prayers to cure those who have been the victim of dwarf-riding (manifested in a high fever that will not break), been attacked by elves or experienced sexual intercourse with the devil (see K. L. Jolly, *Popular Religion in Late Saxon England*, Chapel Hill, NC: University of North Carolina, 1996).

English writing in Anglo-Norman England

If poetry and most prose preserved from Anglo-Saxon England generally displays such clear signs of linguistic, social and religious 'canonicity', the literary communities and the state of English from the Conquest and for a century and more beyond is much harder to summarize. The general impression is of a removal at the Conquest of the ability, or the wish, to maintain the previous intricate techniques in English poetry. This is suggested by the limping meter of poems like that on the death of William the Conqueror in the *Peterborough Chronicle* (under 1087), which was one of the few post-Conquest continuations of the *Anglo-Saxon Chronicle*; it is also suggested by the short post-Conquest poem now called 'The Disuse of English', which in somewhat uneven alliteration lists great 'Englise' writers in order to lament 'Nu is þeo leore forleten, and þet folc is forloren' ('Now is their learning abandoned, and the people lost': in Dickens and Wilson 1969: 2).

The most obvious sign of such 'loss' is in the standards of the language. For nearly a century after the Conquest, many kinds of writings endeavor to maintain versions of the standard written West Saxon. But throughout these writings are signs of abandonment of that standard or reinvention of a new one, and by the twelfth century these are unmistakeable. The earliest 'Middle English' is partly the result of simply allowing scribes to write down the less formal, less 'case-inflected' dialects of English that people had already been using for some time in speech; but once these spoken changes entered writing they led to more pervasive changes, without the restraining power of the earlier written standard. In Anglo-Saxon England's written records, nouns, for instance, take a variety of ways to indicate the plural, depending on the class of noun: *-as*, *-u*, *-e*, *-a*, *-an*, and i-umlaut. By the early eleventh century, the vowels in such final unstressed syllables can all at times be spelled as *e*, indicating a leveling of the vowel sounds in speech, but not necessarily causing further changes in syntax. Once this leveled vowel *-e* was made the written norm in the twelfth century, however, it left only two endings capable of distinguishing between plural and singular: *-es* or *-s*, and *–en* (as in our 'parents' and 'children').

Other changes followed. The genitive singular and plural collapsed together (both became simply *-es*), and other case endings simply fell away, all of which produced a greater need for the kinds of subject-verb-object word order, and for prepositions ('to', 'by' and so forth, instead of a dative or an instrumental case) to show whether a noun is a subject or an object, direct or indirect, or a means by which something occurs. The meanings of some words also changed as Norman French words were added; some word meanings appeared that had probably already been part of spoken usage but were suppressed in the 'classical' written English before the Conquest. The word *drem*, for instance, in formal written English from Anglo-Saxon England exclusively means 'joy, noise, celebration'. But from the twelfth century it also means 'a dream' in the sense of a night-time vision: this probably reflects Old Norse *draumr*, 'a dream'. The word did not acquire a Norse sense suddenly in the twelfth century; rather, that sense most likely dates back to the Viking settlements of the ninth and tenth centuries. The Danish influence from the tenth century on may even have been responsible for more fundamental simplifications and the specifically Norse features that appear in the late-medieval London English, thanks to the north-east's importance to London's wool trade. Thus many notable features of our modern standard English, such as 's' instead of 'th' endings on third-person verbs, pronouns like 'them' and 'their', and the disappearance of most case endings may ultimately derive from Danish farmers who settled, learned English, and became prosperous enough to begin influencing the language of trade and then literature.

There were some continued efforts to retain knowledge of 'classical' pre-Conquest English, as in one remarkable set of distinctive notations from the mid-thirteenth century on manuscripts of Anglo-Saxon prose, especially grammatical treatises, by a Worcester monk whose palsy has earned him the name 'the Tremulous Worcester scribe'. But elsewhere the language developed rapidly and is displayed in a range of regional dialects, none of which could claim to be a national 'standard'. Norman words appeared in English, and, not coincidentally, often concern governance and being governed, such as *justice, prison, masterie* ('mastery'), and *wardein* ('warden'). The kind of French in contact with English shifted in the mid-thirteenth century to words from central France, the region of Paris and the French crown, which from that period on remained constantly within political and literary contacts and aspirations. Central French origins are visible in, for instance, a hard initial /g/ sound instead of Norman French /w/, and a soft initial /ch/ sound instead of Norman French /c/. This left some duplicates: thus English had *wardein* from the Norman Conquest but added *gard*, the same word in central French dialect, in the fifteenth century.

The writings that continued, indeed throve, in English were not the aristocratic, monastic poems but the more 'popular' homilies. These writings, not only the collections by Ælfric and Wulfstan but also less distinguished collections, were the most frequently copied English works in the twelfth century. Always designed for a broad range of people, they present useful moral advice and exhortation, and use literary effects guaranteed to seize listeners' attention rather than requiring the leisure for careful re-reading and decoding, as do many of the 'classical' poems.

From this tradition, and because of its more general religious rather than courtly aristocratic audience and patronage, developed some original genres. One was a dramatically vivid religious prose writing for women religious, the 'Katherine Group' (discussed below under 'English prose in Anglo-Norman England'). This appeared in the Worcester area whose bishop, Wulfstan (not the homilist), was the only Anglo-Saxon bishop to remain in power after the Conquest (d. 1095). Most of the literature in English in this period is for religious men or, especially, women; a religious life was probably an attractive option for women of high Anglo-Saxon lineage, who, as the Latin *Life of Christina of Markyate* (*c*.1160) shows, might need literally to flee into an anchorhold to escape the predatory Norman world.

An exception, however, in its secular focus and perhaps its awareness of Anglo-Saxon poetic traditions is Layamon's *Brut*, also from this time (*c*.1220) and region. This work, the first to present the story of King Arthur in English, is written in what may appear to us as an inconsistent impersonation of Anglo-Saxon alliterative metre, alternating with rhyme and other effects. Perhaps to Layamon this form was an elegant synthesis of literary styles, like the synthesis he achieved in his use of sources. Chiefly using a single French source that was well-known at Henry II's court, Wace's poetic translation (*c*.1170) of Geoffrey of Monmouth's Latin *History of the Kings of Britain* (1137), Layamon nonetheless presents his work in its preface as if it were drawn from a succession of historical writings spanning all the important periods of England's earlier history – the Latin Augustine of Canterbury and St Alban; Bede 'in English' (i.e. a translation); and the French

Wace. His poem shows influences from Ælfric's and Wulfstan's homilies, Latin epic and possibly Welsh as well, but those were literary resources rather than marked as what he claims to be England's monumental writings, none of which is an English poem. His own work, indeed, is preserved in only two copies, one drastically and callously 'modernized'. In contrast, the *Ancrene Wisse*, one of the thirteenth-century religious prose works for women, gained a wide readership and, in adapted forms, was copied into the late fourteenth century (see also p. 77 below).

English literature in later medieval England

The later thirteenth through the mid-fourteenth century brought forth several English works with great ambition and originality as didactic writings, and great importance for expanding the possibilities and claims of English poetry. *The Chronicle* of 'Robert of Gloucester' (*c*.1270) is an ambitious, collaborative, probably monastic verse history of England that includes a vivid account of some contemporary events. *The South English Legendary* (*c*.1280) is a large and engaging collection of lives of saints, preserved in several stages in copies through the first half of the fourteenth century. The *Cursor mundi* (*c*.1300) is a more personally marked and poetically ambitious account of salvation history from Creation to the Harrowing of Hell and then Last Judgement. Finally, the *Pricke of Conscience* (*c*.1350) is a complete manual in verse of basic theological guidance.

These works use elements of a range of 'secular' literature but also put themselves in direct competition with that. *The South English Legendary* begins with the kind of description of spring's return associated with French love poetry, but turns this to religious allegory: the fresh growth 'is oure Cristendom / þat late was on eorþe ysouwe [*sown*] . . . God . . . was þe gardiner' (lines 3–7). So too, the author of the *Cursor mundi* defines his vivid history and quasi-amorous praise of the Virgin in opposition to the poetry of love and chivalry that, he mentions, is so popular with those who seek merely literary 'folly':

Men yernes jestes for to here
And romaunce rede in dyuerse manere
Of Alisaunder þe conqueroure
Of Iulius cesar þe emperoure . . .
In ryot & in rigolage
Spende mony here youþe & her age . . .

Cursor mundi, lines 1–4, 49–50

The cluster of edifying, encyclopaedic and engaging long clerical poems from the early to mid-fourteenth century include two large poems that fully exploit the possibilities of using vivid narrative to offer history and Christian doctrine. Robert Mannynge's *Handlyng Synne* (begun 1303) comprises complex tales illustrating the sins and their branches; his *Chronicle of England* (completed 1338), offers a lively expansion of a French chronicle of English history by Pierre Langtoft.

These poems were written by the clergy for other clergy, but they set the terms for a new range for English poetic authority. While rejecting 'rigolage', all these capacious works allow stories to develop their own details of character, dialogue and surprising plot-twists. At the same time, their doctrinal and ethical frameworks challenge readers to think about the narrative materials in more earnest terms than sheer idle recreation would allow.

These early to mid-fourteenth century long clerical poems set the terms for the acknowledged masterpieces appearing at the century's end. The works by Chaucer, the *Pearl* poet, Gower, Langland and others were no longer 'clerical' in any institutionally confined way; yet they are all learned, continually questioning and continually provocative for political, religious and social thought.

They appear in two basic literary traditions. One is the alliterative style, which appears, or reappears, mostly in the west and north, from Worcester (where Layamon wrote in the early thirteenth century) up into Chester and a span through the north and east into Yorkshire. Just how this tradition, or 'revival', emerged after a lapse of centuries is unclear: it may have been sustained in oral forms, or it may have re-formed the alliterative prose tradition (which was strong in the West) into poetic principles. The visible tradition begins in the mid-fourteenth century with *William of Palerne* (*c.*1360), and continues through *Piers Plowman* in all its versions (*c.*1370–90), the *Wars of Alexander* (*c.*1400), the works of the *Pearl* poet (*c.*1390), the *Siege of Jerusalem* (*c.*1390; more popular than any of the others except for *Piers*), the *Alliterative Morte Arthure* (*c.*1400; used directly by Malory, who there allows his prose to capture some of the effects of alliterative poetry), and many others, copied or composed until late in the fifteenth century, like the '*Gest Hystoriale*' *of the Destruction of Troy* (*c.*1460).

Many of these alliterative poems are historically and socially oriented works; they seem generally in the tradition of a monastic and provincial noble world, rather than the royal one, where French literary forms, meter and actual French poetry predominated. Yet at least some alliterative poetry deals with the court and its French tastes, if from an oblique angle. *Sir Gawain and the Green Knight* spends a remarkable amount of critical attention on the power yet the traps of courtly 'luf-talkyng' and 'frenkysch fare' ('French-style interactions'; lines 927, 1116). Moreover, all the *Pearl* poems (*Sir Gawain and the Green Knight, Cleanness, Patience* and *Pearl*) are remarkable not simply because such fine poems exist, but because they are carefully gathered into a single book, displaying a sense that they ought to be considered a 'kind' of canonical poetry. But even that work, like most of the alliterative poems, exists only in a single copy, unlike the poems from London and the royal court.

That is the other kind of literary tradition of this period, most fully embodied in Chaucer (d. 1400). This is more directly informed by French and even Italian poetry but uses a more eclectic range of style than most French or Italian works, and indeed appears to seek stylistic variety as one of its principles. Chaucer was far from an isolated genius; if any writer was part of a literary community, he was, and he drew many ideas and formal strategies from his London associate John Gower (d. 1408), a master of natural-seeming rhymed narrative. All the London poets of the final decades of

Richard II's reign – Gower (d. 1408), Chaucer and a bold experimenter with the alliterative style, William Langland (? d. 1390) – show aspirations for comprehensive literary form, recalling the large encyclopaedic poems like *Cursor mundi* and *Handlyng Synne* but far exceeding them in generic complexity and hybrid mixtures. Thus William Langland's *Piers Plowman* moves through an enormously ambitious and comprehensive circuit of literary modes and genres to define a kind of sacred history like *Cursor mundi*, but one that opens deeply into the present world and the foibles of the questing narrator amid a succession of allegorical instructors. So too John Gower's *Confessio Amantis*, whose quiet and subtle stories are framed within the 'confession' between an author posturing as a lover and the minion of Venus posturing as a priest, recalls the form of *Handlyng Synne* but collects a vastly more varied range of stories, and frames these ultimately in worldly and civic ethics. Chaucer's *Canterbury Tales* (*c*.1385–1400) outdoes all his peers, however, in ambition for generic variety by presenting a wide compendium of genres connected to a pilgrimage and thus arranged around the cliché that pilgrims were notorious tale-tellers. This allows not only an endlessly provocative juxtaposition of literary forms but also a sense of unending interpretations of and perspective on them, suggested by their story-tellers' commentaries on each other's tales.

Chaucer also exceeds the other fourteenth-century English poets in seeking high literary status in a classical and Continental image, as when he tells his completed poem of *Troilus and Criseyde* to 'kis the steppes' of the great ancient makers of 'poesy', Virgil, Ovid, Homer, Lucan and Statius (5.1790) – and in doing so in fact cunningly imitates Statius's own final address to his *Thebaid* ('do not rival the divine *Aeneid*, but follow after and ever venerate its footsteps' [12.816–17]). To establish this sense of a canon of 'poesy', Chaucer reaches outside English literature because he must, gesturing toward an august poetic tradition that is available to the learned yet not the dogmatically religious, and one that is seemingly sympathetic to women yet which establishes its closest community in an urbane and courtly male perspective. His posture of subservience to great 'poesy', and to great social authority, is understood by his own fifteenth-century followers as a position of establishing a tradition of elegantly modest 'service' that they in turn can follow. By making Chaucer 'the firste fyndere of our fair langage' (Thomas Hoccleve, *Regiment of Princes*, c.1410; line 4978), and the 'cheeff poete of Breteyne' (John Lydgate, *Fall of Princes*, c.1438, Bk. 1, Prol. 247), they manufactured their own authority as continuators of his authoritative gestures of courtly modesty, and in so doing set the terms for centuries of Chaucer's reception (see Carlson 2004, and Chapter 3).

Canons require exclusions, and we can recover some alternatives to Chaucer's kind of poetry better than we can the alternatives to the poetry from Anglo-Saxon England that has come down to us. Chaucer's and Gower's avoidance of Langland's *Piers Plowman* is one kind of exclusion; perhaps ruinously for its contemporaneous literary reputation, that poem was quoted by the Rebels of 1381, whose own literary world is dimly glimpsed through the strange 'letters' that chroniclers collected (see Justice 1994). *Piers* was followed by a small set of political and anticlerical allegories (see below, 'Allegory', under genres), but these altogether miss its delicate poetry and complex self-interrogation. Perhaps *Piers* lacked a real literary following or 'movement' comparable to the Chaucerian one because of the poem's (or poems') extraordinarily original, unclassifiable, multi-generic and constantly revised form. The author's ambitious revisions (the B then the C texts) may have shown everyone that he alone could form his true literary 'school' or following.

The ability of English literature to establish an ethical and dramatic power that relies on no direct clerical uses yet stands above mere adventure and 'rigolage' is the most important 'movement' established by all these later fourteenth-century writers, using alliterative and rhyming forms, in London and the provinces. Just as the earlier clerical long poems in English competed with English entertaining romance, so all the late fourteenth century poets, in London and the alliterative tradition, found ways to reapply both the 'entertaining' romances and the 'useful' clerical English literature that they inherited. Instead of *The South English Legendary*, Chaucer's 'legendary' of saints is *The Legend of Good Women*, a set of tales about virtuous pagan women (and villainous pagan men). Against the serious guidance of confession in the earlier works, Chaucer, Gower, Langland and the *Gawain* poet all present dramatically ironic versions of confession, folding this utilitarian, didactic genre into self-referential, self-exploring worlds. But in a broader perspective the entire span's achievement allows the self-confidence of English literature to bloom widely in the following centuries as it helps allow the laity find serious ethical meaning and intellectual pursuits in the shadow of – but without the direct guidance of – the clergy.

OVERVIEW BY GENRES

This brief and incomplete view of literary communities, movements and forms through these political and cultural periods has noted a number of the genres in English before and after the Conquest. Genre can also serve as a primary category for framing materials and historical periods, allowing us to consider somewhat more precisely the developments and continuities of some notable medieval literary forms across a number of environments.

Epic and historical poetry: Anglo-Saxon England

We often consider the Anglo-Saxon period the great age of the epic. Yet if 'epic' refers to a long written poem treating a purely secular heroic theme and story (although that definition would discount both Homer's *Iliad* and Virgil's *Aeneid*, because both are so oriented to divine forces), then the English poetry of Anglo-Saxon England has left to us only one true epic in anything like a complete form: *Beowulf.* Since that is such a complex, sophisticated and exciting poem, we may count ourselves lucky indeed that it survived mostly intact, although it is very brittle from its scorching in the 1731

Cotton fire (and words that were readable in the early nineteenth century have continued to flake away). *Beowulf* looks back to a world of pagan Danes and Geats, loosely situated in fourth and fifth-century Germanic tribal kingdoms during the period of the Invasions; indeed, *Beowulf* has enough parallels with other Germanic literature to suggest that parts of it spring from long transmissions of pre-Christian mythic history. The Norse prose *Grettírssaga* has a number of parallels, although that was itself not written down until the fourteenth century. Virgil's *Aeneid* presents a similar feeling for how a hero's choices shape a long path of history, but the outcome is the opposite: the *Aeneid* tells of a modern empire's ancient founding, *Beowulf* of a great kingdom's ancient destruction. Whether the *Beowulf* poet knew the *Aeneid* is a tantalizing but unanswerable question.

More broadly, *Beowulf*'s backward look is a crucial element of its culture's version of epic history. The mourners at the end build a monument to Beowulf, and the narrator praises their laments as 'proper'. This sense is contrasted by the view of the pre-Christian northern world as damned to hell: 'Wa bið þæm ðe sceal / þurh sliðne nið sawle bescufan / in fyres fæþm' ('Woe be to those who must thrust their souls in terrible affliction to the [hell]fire's embrace' [183–5]). No one can change the place God has allotted a person or a culture in history, yet the fall of every sparrow must have a divine meaning.

The combination of Christian points and epic style also governs *Exodus*, and, less emphatically, *Andreas*, both of which share a number of lines with *Beowulf*. Indeed, if long poems treating Christian history in heroic terms can be called 'Christian epic', then there are a number of fine examples preserved in complete or mostly complete form: *Juliana*; *Elene*; *Judith*; *Genesis*; *Daniel*; *Christ and Satan*; even the hymnal *Christ* poems. In these, figures from sacred history occupy heroic roles, undergo extraordinary challenges, and face vividly evil enemies (*Judith*, for instance, includes a particularly sharp portrayal of Holofernes, whom Judith decapitates after he has drunkenly had her brought to his tent for a sexual interlude at the end of a banquet).

Somewhere behind all these are lost Germanic oral traditions of historical literature, glimpsed in such scraps as the *Finnsburg Fragment*, recounting an uneasy truce between a band and a group whose leader has been killed (a story that reappears as a 'digression' in *Beowulf*), and the even more fragmentary *Waldere*, whose story of the love and struggles of Walter of Aquitania and Hildegund of Burgundy, who flee the armies of Attila the Hun, is found in a full form in the Latin poem *Walterius* by Ekkehard I of St Gall (d. 973). But behind these too is a long lineage of Latin biblical history cast in epic form: long verse renditions of the story of the Gospels, in which Christianity sought to turn the stylistically rough prose Greek first into Latin prose (in Jerome's translations), then into Latin verse, modeled on Virgil's *Aeneid*. The poetic retelling of the Gospel of Matthew by Juvencus (*c*.330), *Evangeliorum Libri IV*, and that of the Pentateuch by Alcimus Avitus (*c*.500), the *Poematum de Mosaicae Historiae Gestis*, are close relatives to the Anglo-Saxon Christian and non-Christian historical epics.

Short historical poetry that carries the sense of a transcendent set of issues or questions in history can be related to such epic traditions too. The brief poem on the *Battle of Brunanburh*, found in the *Anglo-Saxon Chronicle* under the year 937, frames this victory over a coalition of Norse and Scots as a kind of biblical miracle, in the pattern of Joshua's great battle over five kings at Gabaon; the sun hangs in the sky at Brunanburh long enough for the victory to be complete (lines 13–17) as it did at Gabaon (Jos. 10:13). So too the fragmentary *Battle of Maldon*, describing the fatal choices and final battle of a band of English warriors against some marauding Vikings in 991, seems a meditation, not unlike that of *Beowulf*, on the double-bind of heroic values, rather than a simple historical notice. If for Beowulf the tragedy is that his men finally do not help him when he fights the dragon, for Byrhtnoth in *Maldon* the tragedy is that they finally do, knowing that they are sacrificing themselves.

Closely related to these heroic poems are saints' lives, especially when the saints engage in more or less literal battle with demons. These indeed generally belong among 'historical poetry'. A remarkable poetic example is *Guthlac* (in two sections in the Exeter Book, based on an eighth-century Latin prose version), which includes spectacular attacks by nightmarish demons, including a nearly successful effort to abduct Guthlac to hell, repulsed only by the arrival of St Bartholomew (*Guthlac* 'A', lines 684 ff.). The tradition of prose lives of saints is much larger; see below under 'Prose'.

Epic and historical poetry: Anglo-Norman and later medieval England

Something of this earlier epic spirit, and many elements of its ironic exploration of heroic culture, are continued in Layamon's *Brut*, mentioned above. Here, the story of King Arthur is not the source of scenes of courtly splendour, or love or knightly adventure, as it had already become in many French elaborations; rather, Arthur's tale features heroic failure, and the inability of good rulers to gain wise counsel (and the successful ability of evil ones to gain evil schemes). Layamon's work, like its immediate source, Wace (and ultimately Geoffrey of Monmouth), proceeds far beyond Arthur's own downfall to the destruction of his later people by the Saxon heathens. This historical point has seemed odd for a poem relying on Anglo-Saxon literary forms, but its perspective is fixed on the unrolling of English history through successive conquests and languages, whose centre is the island itself, passed 'from honde to hond' (line 1033).

Historical poetry in English flourishes in so many forms in later medieval England that few major works can be excluded from this category. Certainly Chaucer's *Troilus and Criseyde* (*c*.1386) is 'historical poetry', as is his 'Knight's Tale' (*c*.1380), although in both he seems to shift the larger scope of historical 'great deeds' to the edges (it returns in fuller force in John Lydgate's return to the same stretches of antiquity, in his *Troy Book* [*c*.1420] and his *Siege of Thebes* [*c*.1421], both of which labor in the shadow of Chaucer's two works). Much of the poetry of the 'alliterative revival' from around 1400 (discussed above) is historical. So too are the many romances, discussed below; and so too the even more numerous late medieval poetic saints' lives, considered separately below. That the boundary between 'historical poetry' and these other genres is slight or entirely anachronistic is a sign of the importance of history itself in medieval literature, an importance that is clear from medieval collections. In the Auchinleck Manuscript (*c.*1330), for instance, *Sir Orfeo* and *Horn Child and Maiden Rimnild* bracket *The Anonymous Short English Metrical Chronicle*, and the romance of *Guy of Warwick* follows the list of names of Normans who fought at Hastings known as the *Battle Abbey Roll*. In this last work, halfway through the family names begin to be arranged in rhyming couplets and alternating rhymes, probably for easier memorizing. It is difficult not to see even this quintessentially terse but – in post-Conquest England where many of these families continued to live – richly meaningful list of historical information as chant or poetry.

The lyric: Anglo-Saxon England

All of the short, first-person poems in English before the Conquest whose point is chiefly to portray the speaker's world-weary outlook – *The Seafarer*, *The Wanderer*, *The Wife's Lament*, *The Husband's Message* and *The Ruin* – are found in the late tenth-century monastic volume called the Exeter Book, interspersed with various other kinds of poems. By the simple criteria of being brief poems and in the first person, these are readily classified as 'lyric'. But these poems from the Anglo-Saxon period have a particular quality of renunciation of or despair about the world that distinguishes their voicing from lyric more generally considered. Thus they are usually called 'the Old English elegies', and their similarity of voice and mood is as striking as their variety of details and circumstances.

The Hebrew Bible presents the Psalms, translated into Latin by Jerome in the late fourth century, many of which are laments with some general parallel to the English 'elegies'. Closer, though, to the style of those are the laments or complaints in Celtic and Germanic traditions. In the earliest Welsh (perhaps originally as early as *c.*700) is the poetry of

Llywarch Hen, 'old Llywarch', a collection of observations about the speaker's fall into age, loneliness and despair. In Old Norse, the 'Eddic' poetry preserved from the thirteenth century is also filled with the sort of first-person dialogues and complaints that feature in the English 'elegies'. In Norse too are a number of short laments that seem closer clues to a common genre behind both those and the Anglo-Saxon elegies: *Guðrúnarkviða* (the 'lay of Guthrun') *I*, *II* and *III*, *Helreið Brynhildar*, *Oddrúnargrátr* and *Guðrúnarhvǫt*. These, like the English elegies, are laments by those (in the Norse examples often women) who reflect on their painful and complex circumstances: loss of a beloved, conflict between a lord and kinsman or husband, or both.

Typically, neither the English nor the Norse materials end with an open expectation of an ultimate divine salvation. *The Seafarer* is in that sense exceptional (and in that respect somewhat closer to some biblical psalms). Yet that poem's second half is not crudely spliced onto some pre-Christian 'Germanic' poem, as nineteenth- and early twentieth-century scholars thought; rather, its homiletic Christian ending from line 64 on is well prepared for throughout the poem by a growing sense of how a Christian ethical vision provides a stronger version even than a non-Christian lament might of the narrator's pain and sharp pleasure in exile. The narrator's sense of distance from the comforts of pleasure-loving land-dwellers, dwellers in the cities of the plain, becomes a key to his increasing nearness to God. In relation to much evidence of actual pursuit of religious exile, and the natural detail of the poem, this portrayal is as literal as it is an allegory of the journey through life on earth. Here, a wide range of meanings in exile coexist, and the brevity of the lyric form holds these in a unity as united and unlimited as the sea so vividly presented in the poem.

Medieval Latin provides some literary elaborations of elegiac or complaint poetry, probably ultimately from similar biblical and Germanic mixed literary traditions. One is the lament of the unfortunate woman Radagund of Thuringia, written by Venatius Fortunatus (*c*.600) in the *De excidio*

Thuringiae. As Fortunatus mimes her voice, Radagund tells how she was forced first to live in the household of an uncle who had killed her father the king, then to marry Clothar, king of the Franks, when he conquered Thuringia (in 531), until Clothar allowed her to found a monastery. Her narrative gives a local instance of the kinds of situations that women in the English poetry lament when they serve as 'peace-weavers' between feuding men; the same fate befalls Hildeburh during the feud of Finn, in *Beowulf* (lines 1069–80). Later, still more laments of women are found in literature, from the long twelfth-century Latin poem by Alan of Lille, *The Plaint of Nature*, to the laments of Eve in the Anglo-Norman *Play of Adam*, to the laments of the Virgin in lyrics through the rest of the Middle Ages, to the self-conscious 'compleints' of women in Chaucer. The laments of women in English literature before the Conquest, as in the Finn episode or the enigmatic *The Wife's Lament*, are more haunting because less self-revealing (or less self-indulging). They epitomize the enigmatic ability of the English 'elegies' to present 'studies of situation or emotion applied to imaginary and nameless persons who are detached from any definite associations of time or place' (N. Kershaw, *Anglo-Saxon and Norse Poems*, Cambridge: Cambridge University Press, 1922, p. 6).

Indeed, related to the 'elegies' are the English verse riddles from Anglo-Saxon England, a further form of short first-person poem, and thus a species of lyric in the broadest sense. As the doubts about the narrator's identities in the 'elegies' suggest, a riddling outlook is endemic to Anglo-Saxon English poetry. *The Dream of the Rood* is, indeed, directly paralleled by at least two Latin riddles. A long lineage of such Latin riddles spans the Middle Ages: terse, witty works making puzzles with language as well as concepts and scriptural history, collected in the Anglo-Saxon period in groups known as the riddles of pseudo-Bede, *Adrian and Ritheus*, and a group collected by the early eighth-century writer Tatwine, contemporary of Bede.

The Exeter Book presents all 95 known English riddles from Anglo-Saxon England; these are clearly, like the other works in that volume, pieces designed for learned monks who had probably often been aristocratic, or who certainly had frequent connections to the broader Anglo-Saxon aristocratic and royal world. The riddles are not explicitly religious; indeed they are perhaps the least religious works in all of Anglo-Saxon writing. Their focus is on the playful power of language to create misleading suggestions, to evoke possible 'meanings' by clues that then are shown not at all to be the meaning 'really' meant. Sex, food, insects and other homely and quite secular matters are suggested allusively in the riddles, even when the 'solutions' point to a quite different direction: books, keys, bread-dough, bows.

Those correct 'answers' are all, to be sure, the proper domain of monks. The clues, however, show the breadth of worldly knowledge that the monastic world in this period could contain and transmit. The Exeter riddles thus suggest better than many other kinds of literature how easily a poem like *Beowulf*, or indeed much more whimsical creativity, might have prospered in the Anglo-Saxon monastic world. A strange monster is described, whose beak digs into the ground, snuffling, while his lord and guardian, stooping, walks on his tail; a wooden point is driven through his back, and he leaves a trail that is green on one side and dark on the other. We can solve that one (no. 26) as a 'plough', but we are vividly instructed in more than monastic farming implements by the mental process of doing so. Such works show a play of mind that is acutely visual, and much attuned to the possibilities of another world, but one less of Christian heaven than of the kinds of strange creatures that frame the borders or stare from the first letters in the eighth-century Irish *Book of Kells* as well as other Irish-influenced manuscripts of early Northumbrian culture.

The lyric: Anglo-Norman and late medieval England

After the Conquest the English lyric occupies a much wider range of forms. Its basis in 'plot' and aspirations seems more clearly secular and courtly, but those resources are applied at least as often to religious topics. In every Western European language from the twelfth century on emerge short, meta-phorically rich, songlike poems about the love of, or directly expressing love to, a beloved or admired other – earthly or divine, sexual or sacred, or even love of a place or a ruler. Its sources are various. The Greek lyric tradition was lost to the Middle Ages except that absorbed into Latin lyrics by the Roman poets, who in turn continued to be read in medieval learned culture (especially Horace and Virgil), and who helped inspire perhaps the richest tradition of lyric in the Middle Ages, the medieval Latin lyrics, by authors from Boethius and Alcuin to a vast range of named and anonymous authors in the twelfth and later centuries. Vernacular lyrics draw from the Latin tradition, sometimes directly, but also from a wide range of more immediate sources and contexts, in the everyday course of using song and poetry to celebrate reverence, love, desire, loss and renewal.

The English lyric appears thinly just after the Conquest: the short poem 'Durham' (c.1080), praising those Anglo-Saxon saints buried in Durham Cathedral, continues the tradition of pre-Conquest English verse forms; a brief hymn to the Virgin by Godric of Finchale from the mid-twelfth century is the first English lyric in the verse forms modeled on the French lyric (although this hymn recalls Latin hymns more than French love poetry). The English lyric displays increasingly abundant development and preservation in the thirteenth, and especially the fourteenth and fifteenth centuries. The lyric is often anonymous, but Chaucer and Gower both produced excellent examples, the latter in Latin and French as well as English; in the fifteenth century, Thomas Hoccleve (d. 1426), John Lydgate (d. 1449), and Charles of Orleans (d. 1465), are all followers of Chaucer's patterns of literature and of the many great French lyricists of the fourteenth century, such as Guillaume de Machaut (d. 1377), Eustache Deschamps (d. 1407), and Jehan Froissart (d. 1412), better known to modern readers for his chivalric prose chronicle. From the French tradition the English authors learned ways of connecting lyrics or locating them within larger works, and of using personification allegory in them, holding an elaborate funeral and inquest after the death of Pity, for instance, as Chaucer does; or connecting a series of personal, lyric 'compleints' into a large single narrative, as Hoccleve does.

Beyond the courtly writers and followers of courtly lyrics, the English religious lyric is a more pervasive and fugitive genre, found tucked in sermons and the margins of other texts and hymns, and, rarely, found collected together with secular lyrics in medieval collections of lyrics such as Digby MS 86 and Harley MS 2253 (made, respectively, in the late thirteenth and the first quarter of the fourteenth century). Many more religious than courtly English lyrics were produced in the later Middle Ages. Both are highly crafted. The many lyrical impersonations of the Virgin poignantly comforting her baby who will grow up and die are as self-consciously artful as the brief lyric lament by a jilted female lover, who tells her sad story of why 'I go with childe, wel I wot; / I schrew the fadur þat hit gate [*who conceived it*]'. Some lyrics were probably written by real women (the most likely group of these is in the 'Findern' manuscript, Cambridge University Library MS Ff. 1.6, from the fifteenth and sixteenth centuries), but impersonation of a woman's lamenting voice is a lyricist's stock in trade. The single copy of the fifteenth-century lament by the jilted pregnant woman is signed at the end, 'bryan hys [*is*] my name iet' (Robbins 1952, no. 23).

Prose: Anglo-Saxon England

Although prose invariably develops later than poetry in any literature, it is visible from an early period in Anglo-Saxon England, thanks in large part to the translations of Latin prose works that King Alfred sponsored. This prose includes a wide range of genres: the *Anglo-Saxon Chronicle*, saints' lives, homilies, scientific or cosmological writing and other kinds. As noted above, the 'Alfredian' prose also includes the important and original English translations of early Christian Latin writings by such authors as Augustine, Gregory the Great, Boethius, Orosius and Bede. Short notices of saints' lives appear in the prose English *Martyrology* (*c*.900), a more popular work than the other English prose except for the translation of Bede; longer prose saints' lives appear in significant numbers in the eleventh century, especially by Ælfric, but also in a large number of separate and anonymous copies.

The homilies are often rhetorically powerful compositions. Ælfric offers a quiet and lucid rhythmic chant; his balanced, not fully alliterating lines present nearly an equivalent to blank verse. Wulfstan, renowned as the best preacher of his time, is less finely intellectual but particularly capable of a hammering, vivid denunciation, as in the brilliant 'Sermon of the Wulf' (1014), which achieves a satiric style evoking the Roman satirist Juvenal as much as the Hebrew prophet Jeremiah (both of which were readily available as models). But Wulfstan, like Ælfric, fully inhabits his prose with his own recognizable style; their differences are clear even when Wulfstan remakes a homily from Ælfric, as in his expansion of Ælfric's 'De falsis deis' ('On false gods').

Prose: Anglo-Norman England

The prose English homily persisted from Anglo-Saxon to Anglo-Norman England – indeed, it is one of the best 'linking' genres between the periods. As noted above (p. 57), more English homilies from Anglo-Saxon England are copied in the twelfth century than before the Conquest, often mixed with more recent homilies. But other kinds of prose used in Anglo-Saxon England ceased at the Conquest, or were fundamentally changed. No complete translations of ancient histories appeared like that of Orosius from the ninth century until the late fourteenth century, when John Trevisa translated Methodius (*c*.1388); Boethius was not translated into English until Chaucer's *Boece* (*c*.1380); no complete translations of patristic theology like Bishop Waerferth of Worcester's translation of Gregory the Great's *Dialogues* or Alfred's translation of Augustine's *Soliloquia* appeared until the fifteenth century, and the translations of theology then were of more recent medieval materials. The *Dialogues* were not themselves translated again until 1608, the *Soliloquia* not until 1624 (P. W., *The Dialogues of S. Gregorie, surnamed the Greate*, Paris, 1608; A. Batt, *A heavenly treasure of confortable meditations and prayers written by S. Augustin*, S Omer, 1624, pp. 189ff.).

Lacking the earlier sponsorship for so wide a range, English prose in the Anglo-Norman period (from *c.*1100 to 1250) nonetheless developed some genres from Anglo-Saxon England into entirely new forms. The *Peterborough Chronicle*, in its first part a version of the *Anglo-Saxon Chronicle*, recopied in its entirety in the eleventh century from another monastery's copy when the original at Peterborough Abbey burned, but continued until the accession of Henry II in 1154, shows the pressures but also the possibilities of new circumstances on the kind of historical prose from Anglo-Saxon England. Apart from some obvious twelfth-century insertions into the earlier, recopied sections from Anglo-Saxon England – especially stories proclaiming the wondrous discovery of charters that spell out Peterborough Abbey's 'ancient' rights in terms that might have seemed necessary during the national disruptions of the mid-twelfth century – the chronicle otherwise continues for a time in the vein of the pre-Conquest *Anglo-Saxon Chronicle*, in regular units of years with important national events plus some related or unrelated intriguing narratives. But the Peterborough chronicler's short-lined, rhymed poetic paean on the occasion of the death of William I, whom the writer, in a rare personal reference, claims to have seen once at court, is very far from Anglo-Saxon alliterative poetic traditions. Lacking its traditional impersonal authority, the *Anglo-Saxon Chronicle* becomes personal.

By the early twelfth century, under another writer at Peterborough, the chronicle presses this change in form and focus more drastically: it becomes a detailed and passionately opinionated account of local and national events, moving between satirical accounts of the unctuously ambitious Norman abbot who convinced King Henry II to give him control of Peterborough Abbey, to a bitter denunciation of the torments of the common people under King Stephen during the 'Anarchy' (partly quoted in the previous chapter).

Such historical prose, while it increasingly bespeaks a sense of cultural isolation, also increasingly unfolds a local, idiosyncratic and moody perspective, whose complexity would be disallowed by the stately accounts of the pre-Conquest parts of the *Anglo-Saxon Chronicle* as completely as the new idiomatic turns of language that appear in the *Peterborough Chronicle* would be prohibited from the formal English of the chronicle before the Conquest.

A highly local audience is also partly responsible for the subtlety and intimacy of the prose 'Katherine Group', *c.*1200, a set of prose saints, lives of Saints Margaret, Katherine and Juliana that achieve a degree of drama, including dialogue that might well have been acted out, far more vividly than do the lives in the Anglo-Saxon prose *Martyrology* with which the writer is clearly familiar. In the same dialect is a prose work, *Hali Meithhad* ('Holy Virginity'), that argues the case for women to find spiritual and intellectual freedom from men and the world by choosing a celibate religious life. Within this narrow focus of celibacy appears the first extended discussion in English of 'freedom' as a social ethic, even an innate right.

This manifesto for the spiritual and intellectual freedom of the chaste religious life is in keeping with the emphasis on the political rights and freedoms appearing at the same time in the Latin Magna Carta. So too in Geoffrey of Monmouth's *History of the Kings of Britain* appears in a speech by the Britons to the Romans a similar proclamation of a people's rights of liberty – a topic that had also appeared in twelfth-century canon law (see A. Galloway, 'Writing history in England', in Wallace, ed. (1999), p. 267). This topic is no less augustly presented in the English manifesto on women's power to choose religious celibacy. The domestic scale of the terms, however, defines every aspect of English prose of this period. In the same elegant western dialect, and found in one of the same copies, is an allegorical portrayal of the proper 'custody of the soul' (*Sawles Warde*): here, the soul is a household that must be well managed by the husband Wit (Reason), whose domestic preparations are dramatically presented in his conversations with his doorkeeper Warschipe (Prudence) and her virtuous sisters Meath (Temperance) and Rihtwisnesse (Justice), as they receive a special visitor with an important message, Fealac, Deathes sonde (Fear, Death's messenger). Most ambitious of these thirteenth-century English prose works is the *Ancrene Wisse*, a large and elegant guide for the women who enclosed themselves as anchoresses in the cells of churches for the rest of their lives. The writer appeals to his enclosed readers in metaphors and language that affectionately invoke but reinterpret the elements of French romance, the natural reading material for their secular counterparts: Christ is like a yearning and heroic knight, who fights against the devil for his lady in a castle, but she is so hard-hearted that she allows him to die without letting him in. Elsewhere the writer says that God gives his love freely, but in return he also snatches his human beloved's favors – like an impatient lover or even a rapist who will not be denied: 'Answer now, and protect yourself against me if you can! Or else give me your love that I long for so intensely – but not for my own, but rather your great benefit' ('Ondswere nu ant were the, yef thu const, ayein me, other yette me thi luve the ich yirne se swathe – nawt for min ah for thin ahne muchele biheve' [pt. 7, lines 192–4]). Here too the issue of 'freedom' is prominent, but paradoxical, with the bondage to God yielding freedom from the world. That paradox continues into subtle use of literary genre: the *Ancrene Wisse* is throughout entwined in the images and plot elements of romance, from which it frees itself only by means of a fuller dramatization of romance features.

Prose: later medieval England

The tendency of English prose in Anglo-Norman England to be crafted for women continued with the many passionate religious treatises by Richard Rolle (died 1349, probably from the Black Death that arrived that year), followed by many other religious writings in prose. Such religious prose proliferates in the fourteenth and fifteenth centuries, from quasi-rapturous

Crucifixion imagery like Rolle's 'Meditation on the Passion' (*c*.1340), to full allegories of spiritual activities and outlooks like the *Abbey of the Holy Ghost*, to deftly and lucidly controlled instructions for meditation like Walter Hilton's late fourteenth-century *Scale of Perfection* (both *c*.1390). By the end of the fourteenth century and the turn of the fifteenth, two writers of religious English prose were themselves women: Julian of Norwich and, speaking in the third person and purportedly using a sequence of male scribes for her dictation, Margery Kempe. But by this time religious prose in general was not only for women, nor primarily for those who had chosen a professional religious life. Such prose was written for those men and women following the 'mixed life' (as another treatise by Hilton called this), seeking a spirituality amenable to active, lay Christians, who might be deeply part of family, guild and civic life but still sought opportunities for cultivating personal spiritual experience.

Also extending the tradition of religious English prose for the laity were the writings of the Lollards. Here, moral instruction that assumes lay self-sufficiency is mixed with outright anticlerical polemic. Appearing from the late fourteenth century, Lollard prose includes the most ambitious set of English sermons in the period, and by 1395 a full translation of the Bible, which attained a wide and often entirely orthodox readership (see above, p. 39). But after the suppression of the Lollards, much of the religious prose tradition of the fifteenth century was explicitly keyed to inculcating orthodoxy, including Nicholas Love's *Mirror of the Blessed Life of Jesus Christ* (*c*.1410), a very popular English translation of an equally popular Latin work (falsely attributed to St Bonaventure) describing how to conjure and meditate on sacred history in the imagination.

Love's work influenced late medieval sacred drama as well as private meditation, and even this suggests the public realm to which English prose now laid claim. Other prose had still greater claims to aristocratic and public authority. In 1387, the Oxford-educated chaplain (and friend of John Wyclif) John Trevisa translated a long, nearly contemporary Latin 'universal' history, by the monk Ranulph Higden. This was the first full English translation of any massive Latin work since the period of King Alfred, and its appearance marks a change in the prestige of English prose, a change that Trevisa recognizes and carefully orchestrates in the 'Dialogue' appended as introduction to the translation. There, Trevisa cunningly has a 'Knight' (who resembles his patron, Sir Thomas Berkeley) vigorously prove to a reluctant 'Clerk' that there is a universal need for an updated world history in English. An aristocratic, masculine and public authority could not be more explicitly inscribed in the making of English prose.

Prose alone can wield administrative power, and it was long associated with a higher claim than verse to 'truth' in historical writing. The casting of English in this role in the early fifteenth century generally indicates its confirmed public authority. Henry V's use of English in all of his correspondence from 1417 to 1422, including his letters from France describing the progress of the war, are an important turning point both in English and in English prose, as well as in the establishing of a particular set of standard features. From 1450 English is routinely used in parliamentary records and most other public records. At roughly the same time Sir John Fastolf commissioned a translation of the prose *Dicts and Sayings of the Philosophers*, a compilation of ancient authorities. That work was translated again in 1473 by Anthony Wydeville, second Earl Rivers, brother of King Edward IV's wife Elizabeth; the work was the first book printed in England (by Caxton in *c*.1475, just before Caxton first printed Chaucer's *Canterbury tales*).

By the first half of the fifteenth century, historical prose emerged in hundreds of copies of the *Brut*, a prose English translation of a French prose translation of the history of England. This was based in its early sections on the stories of King Arthur that had come down in their first full form from the twelfth century in Geoffrey of Monmouth's Latin *Deeds of the British Kings*, but it was continued into contemporary political history in the fourteenth and fifteenth centuries. The prose *Brut* was practically a family Bible in many a gentry household, with generations of the names of owners on most copies. Next to the Wycliffite Bible, it is the most demonstrably popular work in English of the Middle Ages.

The Arthurian tradition of such prose writing came to a particularly fine point with Thomas Malory's antiquarian tales about the knights of the Round Table (*c*.1460). Malory's prose revives the tradition of epic in something like its original spirit: an earnestly nostalgic and sweeping tour of a lost heroic world, yet one that further substantiated the place of English prose in an aristocratic, public and – in a world of brutal political struggle dominated more clearly than ever by men – masculine social sphere.

Romance: later medieval England

In its root sense, 'romance' refers to sources in Latin. When English writers use the term, however, they are often referring to tales in French; and the genre does not, therefore, appear in England until after the Conquest, or, indeed, until after the blooming of the French chivalric romances in the twelfth and thirteenth centuries. Thanks to an important collection, the Auchinleck manuscript (*c*.1330), English verse romances are known from the period of *Cursor mundi*, which, as noted above, roundly condemns them in its preface; they continued to be widely copied in the fifteenth century and printed in the sixteenth.

The distinction of some tales as 'romance' rather than 'history' is sometimes hard to specify in absolute terms, since either kind of writing could involve stories about giants, demons, knightly 'aventure' and relatively recent or distant historical figures; either can be in verse or, by the fifteenth century, prose. The tales of King Arthur and his knights particularly waver between these genres. Even Arthurian works defined as histories seemed to collect fantastic elements, especially in their descriptions of early or foundational moments of history. The prose *Brut*, a reliable source for military and social history in its fourteenth-century sections, begins in many copies with the tale of Diocletian and his fifty daughters, who murder their fifty husbands on their wedding nights and are exiled to Britain where they copulate with demons and produce a race of giants that Brutus, the grandson of Aeneas, has to conquer before he can found England. Works of 'history', however, usually continue or are meant to continue to the present; the term romance should mostly be reserved for the verse narratives that present distant, usually exotic worlds, where love, disguise, exile, reunion and some re-founding of society or a particular family or kingdom shape the accounts. Their settings or 'matter' include antiquity (especially Thebes and Troy, and Alexander's battles), English history (from Arthur and his knights, to Athelstan and his, including Guy of Warwick and other English figures), and 'crusades' or orientalizing narratives (often using Roland and Charlemagne, but also other figures from chronicles or legends).

All such works can move between a range of values and genres, and serve a variety of uses. The elusive 'truth-status' of such materials is often part of its interest, and its utility for various purposes. Neither wholly verifiable nor wholly fanciful, the stories in romance materials seem more than most medieval traditions to exceed any definitive classification by genre. Romances treating relations between Christians and Muslims ('Saracens') particularly waver at the horizon of history, fancy and moral tale. The verse *The King of Tars* (*c*.1330), for instance, tells of a Christian maiden who, under duress, marries a Muslim ('Saracen') sultan and appears to adopt his religion (although she secretly remains Christian). Impregnated by him, she gives birth to a lump of flesh, but she is able to prove that it can be transformed to a well-proportioned child by the baptism of a Christian priest whom the Sultan has imprisoned. The miracle converts her husband, who himself turns from black to white, then in turns forces his people to be converted or die; many joyously do, though others are executed. This poem appears amid a series of 'romances' and historical writing in the Auchinleck manuscript, but another copy is found amid moral instruction, saints' lives and didactic poetry in the Vernon and Simeon manuscripts. Is it a 'romance'? Furthermore, its basic story appears in several early fourteenth-century Latin chronicles (although there it does not include the brutal form of conversion of the king's people, one way in which the poem is more 'historically' oriented than the chronicles). Its plot resembles Chaucer's *Man of Law's Tale*, itself adapted from a story in a French prose chronicle by Nicholas Trevet (*c*.1340) that otherwise constitutes carefully dated and widely accepted historical materials.

This wavering on the edge of 'history' may explain why English romances are often less 'courtly', and more 'historical' or 'magical', than the French versions. Beginning with *King Horn* and *Havelok* from the late thirteenth or early fourteenth century, and continuing through *Ipomedon* (in verse and prose) in the fifteenth century, English romances tend to emphasize political background and military action over the psychological conflicts and emphasis on women's passions found in their French originals. Legal issues are often more highlighted, and the tone, detail and plot can seem to affirm a lower social caste than the aristocratic world of the French romance literature. In *Havelok*, the king begins his career as an urban day-labourer, and in *Richard Coer de Lyon* the king enjoys shaming overly delicate French aristocrats who will not stoop to dirty their hands as the king does in a public task. The Duke of Burgundy recoils from helping Richard build a city wall because, the Duke snobbishly says, 'My fadyr nas [*was not*] mason ne carpentere' (5955–6044).

Yet 'social realism' in the English romances is often balanced by magic, as in *Sir Orfeo* (*c*.1330) or *Sir Gawain and the Green Knight* (*c*.1390), or indeed the wondrous and violent deeds of King Richard the Lionheart, and many others. Such an emphasis on miracle and 'wonder' gives English romance its occasion to depart from at least most kinds of history, yet the genre often uses its freedom to present unsettling views of familiar social issues.

Saints' lives: later medieval England

The genre of saints' lives in Anglo-Saxon and Anglo-Norman England has been mentioned already under 'Epic and historical poetry: Anglo-Saxon England' and 'Prose'. Late medieval English saints' lives in verse, which draw on French, Latin and local English sources, are a more varied body of materials. They are sometimes but a short step from the romances; Guy of Warwick, for instance (the English verse *c.*1440 is based on an Anglo-Norman French poem *c.*1250), ends his life as a pilgrim (who returns to fight and win one last time) whom an angel finally draws up to heaven. The venerable genre of the saint's life can also be seen as an original vehicle for some of romance elements that bloom later. Certainly, the ninth-century Latin, then twelfth-century Anglo-Norman French *Voyage of St Brendan*, which includes a conversation with Judas perched on a rock in the ocean, briefly allowed to cool his face from the heat of hell's flames, is magical enough to qualify, as are the stories of St Ursula and the eleven thousand virgins, or the story of St Thomas of Becket with its account of his father's marriage to a beautiful Saracen princess, who manages to find him in England in spite of her ignorance of English. All three of these accounts are included in the English *South English Legendary* (*c.*1280), with nearly 90 others. Many of the lives of English saints there, such as St Kenelm, have particularly curious stories that represent traditions springing directly from local cults and their legends rather than Latin continental materials shaped by centuries of editing and official review, especially via Jacob of Voragine's enormously widespread *Golden Legend* (*c.*1260).

Fifteenth-century England offers a renewed burst of English production of traditional saints' lives, especially by such authors as Osbern Bokenham (d. 1447), John Lydgate (d. 1449), and John Capgrave (d. 1464). As the prefaces of their works sometimes say, many of these verse lives were written at the direction of aristocratic women. It is clear that the genre of the saint's life, which Chaucer adapts both in the

Second Nun's Tale and *The Legends of Good Women*, was very popular indeed, a popularity further supported by the translation of the *Golden Legend* into English, as the *Gilte Legende* (1438). Apart from the malcontent Lollards, fifteenth-century popular tastes show no sign of the utter rejection of worship of saints that would follow in the Reformation.

Allegory in the later Middle Ages

Allegory involves a representation of ideas or abstract entities, usually in personifications whose actions and speech are significant ways to understand those ideas, or, sometimes, to contradict or test them. The Latin tradition begins with Prudentius's influential *Psychomachia* (*c*.405), where virtues and vices clash in a detailed battle; but it also begins simply with Christian theology, whose ideas provide many materials for dramatic realization. Anglo-Saxon English writing presents debates between the 'body and soul' in two poems, and King Alfred's translation of Boethius's *Consolation of Philosophy*, which he turned from an allegorical lesson by Philosophy and Boethius into a debate between 'Wisdom' and 'Mod' ('mind'). But otherwise few English poems before the Conquest are explicitly allegorical. Only with the twelfth century, when an effusion of elaborate Latin allegorical poetry by Alan of Lille appeared, do first French, then English authors begin to offer poetry based on the premise of personified ideas or principles, usually in some thematically significant dramatic action.

That action is often simply a debate or series of lessons, the most common 'plot' for allegorical poetry in Latin, French and English. The most influential of all medieval vernacular poems, the French *Roman de la Rose* (1235–75) owes much to Alan of Lille's poems, and much of it is a series of lessons by such figures as False Seeming, Fair Welcome and Nature. All later English (and French) allegory, including the most elaborate instance, *Piers Plowman* (*c*.1370–90), draws directly or indirectly from the *Rose* or its French followers; like it, many are in the form of dream-visions. Leaving aside the extraordinarily original *Piers Plowman*, English poetry created some home-grown varieties of allegory: the short alliterative *Winner and Waster* (*c*.1360) is a colloquial but complex, balanced and unresolved debate between figures personifying two economic modes: hoarding and spending; this poem may have influenced *Piers Plowman*, which has a major debate between Meed (money) and Conscience. *The Parliament of Three Ages* (*c*.1380) is a vision of characters embodying the different ages of life, framed as a dream-vision by a poacher who awakens aware of his own mortality.

Although the *Roman de la Rose* probably influenced *Piers Plowman*, perhaps directly, the lessons in *Piers* are antithetical to the courtly, leisured, sexual world of the *Roman*. That world is spurned in favor of a difficult quest to define the ethical life, and *Piers* ends not with the taking of the sexualized 'castle' as in the *Roman*, but with the building of a sanctuary called 'Unity', although that is breached and destroyed just as the castle in the *Roman*, with directly sexual meaning, is breached and set aflame. The bulk of allegory continued to follow the secular values and whimsical modes of the *Rose*; a small group of followers of *Piers*, however, developed its allegory for political, supposedly anti-courtly criticism: *Richard the Redeless* (*c*.1420), *Mum and the Sothsegger* (*c*.1450), and, less directly, *The Crowned King* (*c*.1450). Another alliterative follower of *Piers Plowman*, *Pierce the Ploughman's Crede* (*c*.1460), presents anticlerical satire, a close relative of allegory and found throughout the *Rose* as well, since satire describes 'types' in action much as allegory does.

English satire: Anglo-Saxon to late medieval England

Christian ethics require denunciation of sin (Leviticus 19:17; Galatians 2:11–14; 2 Peter 2:15–16), and homilies in Anglo-Saxon England, especially those by Wulfstan, express this privilege forcefully. Anglo-Saxon England also knew the Latin satires of Juvenal and of Ovid. But the great age of poetic Latin satire occurs after the Conquest, in the twelfth- and thirteenth-century 'goliardic' Latin poems by Walter of Chatillon, Hugh Primas, and the massive anonymous collection known as the *Carmina Burana*, along with many other poems by 'Golias', the name given collectively to the many anonymous poems of this kind. French satire followed close behind, sometimes as expanded translations of the Latin, like the French translation of the satirically misogynist twelfth-century *Lamentations* by Matheolus. The influential, thirteenth-century French *Roman de la Rose*, especially its second part by Jean de Meun, established a means by which satire developed into allegorical forms; and this fusion – followed up by many more frenetically satirical French allegories, such as the fourteenth-century *Roman de Fauvel* – is followed in late medieval English satire as well.

'Estates satire' refers to a conspectus of the ideals of the social estates and contemporary departures from those ideals; poems in this vein hold a major position in Latin, French and then English materials, with Chaucer, Gower and Langland, all of whom present such a genre, more or less obviously, in their 'prologues'. The background of estates satire to Chaucer's *General Prologue* is deliberately hidden; the portraits are made to seem the purely individual figures that the narrator has by chance encountered; their pervasive condition of delusion and self-interest, or at least self-righteous self-consciousness, is all the more devastatingly clear. 'How shal the world be served?' Chaucer's narrator seems to hear, approvingly, his Monk impatiently ask those who would keep him obedient to his traditional monastic principles. The more direct condemnation of the sins of the modern social orders in Langland's and Gower's prologues is, however, no less complex and innovatively ironic. Langland, for instance, not only skewers a greater social range than Chaucer; he also makes his own narrator more clearly the object of satire and criticism throughout his poem. Langland's persona Will is often displayed as misguided in his addresses to authoritative allegories (such as Reason and Conscience, in passus 5 of the C text). *Piers Plowman* thus directly explores the ethical difficulties of the satirist as well as of the world he satirizes.

So does Gower, in another way. Although his long French and longer Latin poems, the *Mirour de l'Omme* (*c.*1378) and *Vox clamantis* (*c.*1382), are both dedicated to denouncing the abuses of a wide range of social estates, and thus qualify as 'satire' in the medieval social vein, his English poem, the *Confessio Amantis*, which begins with another estates satire, moves beyond that posture to scrutinize throughout the motives and delusions of the narrator, Amans (the 'Lover'). Only when this figure turns out to be old John Gower after all, with no capacity for sexual love and its delusions, can he achieve a voice of moral advice that is not fraught with the potential for hypocrisy, for condemning in others what he is committing himself. Chaucer avoids that possibility by leaving his own response to the sins of the estates uncertain: it is impossible that he is indeed as approving of them all as he seems, but he nowhere risks standing forth as a direct critic of a narrowly self-interested, professionalized mode of society for whose failings he could indeed be interrogated.

The late fourteenth-century social satirists find many ways acutely to transform the genre of satire under the bright light of keen ethical awareness. Yet social satire is always less stable in Christian culture, with its emphasis on personal motives and the question of a writer's sin or grace, than it is in the ancient materials from Juvenal and Ovid on which it is originally based. It always carries the potential for hypocrisy, and thus tends to encourage some or much self-parody, as in the Latin 'goliardic' satires.

Drama: Anglo-Saxon to late medieval England

Beyond and around what we can readily classify as 'drama', and indeed surrounding all medieval literature, is a large and long tradition of Easter liturgy, in Latin, presented by and chiefly to religious professionals, around and within a church altar in the very early hours of Easter morning or the days preceding, focusing on a few key scenes before and after the Crucifixion and using for what can barely be called 'stage props' a life-size cross, a thurifer (or censer, a smoking container of 'purifying' incense), and a shroud. Monks crouch in the 'tomb' to recite (and sing) the words of the angel telling the three Marys (who are other monks, dressed as the three women seeking the crucified Jesus as in Luke 23:55–24:6) that 'He is not here, but has arisen'. The darkened church is then lit with sudden candlelight and the celebration of Easter, and the forty days of severe abstinence during Lent are over.

We would call this ritual. Yet even the most liturgically oriented drama can bloom into complex productions that merge readily into what we might call 'history plays' (or at least 'sacred history plays'), complete with stirring solo performances (often accompanied by music, thus more like opera than spoken drama), subtle attention to representations of the historical past and a great variety of set-pieces from other genres. Sometimes church drama becomes truly grandiose, especially in continental twelfth-century plays of 'Daniel' and of the Passion. But often a remarkable power is generated from relatively simple elements of production. In Anglo-Saxon England, in the late tenth century (that is, during a time of particular efforts to standardize the liturgy and reform the rules guiding the monastic way of life) appeared a particularly delicate and powerful production of the Adoration of the Cross, the Interment of the Cross in the Sepulchre and the three Marys' Visit to the Sepulchre, in the *Regularis Concordia*. Such powerful liturgical drama continued through the fifteenth century; Katherine Sutton, abbess of the nunnery of Barking just outside London (a short distance from Chaucer's everyday world, but a long way from his parody of such women religious in his fatuous Prioress), energetically rewrote the Easter liturgical drama *c.*1375 for her nuns, adding elaborate action and speeches, including kissing the empty place of the Crucifix and pouring real wine and water poured over the wounds of the carved crucified Jesus, 'to quicken the devotion of the faithful' (Young 1933, vol. 1: 164; vol. 2: 411).

A more self-sufficiently 'fictional' kind of sacred drama is recorded in England soon after the Norman Conquest, in the densely creative French twelfth-century *Jeu d'Adam* (*Play of Adam*). This presents vivid characters of Adam, Eve, God, the Devil, Cain and Abel, plus a contemporary 'Jew', a plant in the audience, who rises up to challenge vigorously the Old

Testament patriarchs and prophets announcing the hints of the Incarnation in the Hebrew Bible. This breaches historical boundaries deliberately, and engagingly, showing the living power of the drama (the young 'Jewish' challenger from the audience is convinced, and converts). The full exploitation of the power of sacred drama to define a separate world of sacred history, and then to breach that separation, appears in English in the early fifteenth century, with the productions of 'Cycle' plays presenting all of sacred history on the midsummer feast of Corpus Christi. The four preserved full cycles of such drama, from Creation to Domesday, combine a wide array of genres, effects and provocative connections between sacred history and the contemporary world.

In these productions, the framework of 'salvation history', mounted by the guilds of major cities (but not apparently London), allows a range of genres: from fabliau (old Joseph and a pregnant young Mary), tragedy (Abraham and Isaac, Herod, the Crucifixion) to comedy (the Second Shepherds' Play). These plays produce a carefully cultivated effect not only of remaking past history into the form of the present, but also of showing that the present has the potential to become sacred history. The Wakefield play of *The Salutation of Elizabeth to Mary* is a remarkable example. There, the everyday greetings or 'salutations' of two fifteenth-century East Anglian townswomen contain, with complete naturalness, the potent liturgical words of the *Ave* ('Hail Mary . . . '). If such a key moment of sacred history can emerge from everyday speech, then everyday speech is itself shown to be full of the power to create the sacred.

Not all the theatrical entertainment was of this overtly edifying kind, of course; jesters and mimes have an ancient lineage, dimly visible when their antics appear in civic documents or in the Anglo-Norman *Play of Adam*, where devils race around Adam and Eve 'grimacing appropriately' ('gestum facientes competentem'). Something of a tradition of more crudely farcical entertainment is visible in the early thirteenth-century English *Interludium de Clerico et Puella*, the oldest secular play in English (ed. Bennett and Smithers 1974: 196–200). Here, an old woman's trick of making a dog weep from mustard spice allows a cleric to convince a young girl that she should have sexual relations with him or face his revenge: he has the power to turn any woman who denies his advances into an animal, like the last girl who tried that.

Secular kinds of drama appear framed within moral drama. In the fifteenth century, professional acting troops were likely responsible for such masterpieces as *Mankind*, where Latin pomposity is ridiculed even as clerical power is superficially asserted; the commercial basis for the play is brought into the work itself by having the monstrous Titivullus collect the money from the crowd. Other fifteenth-century professional works like the grotesque *Croxton Play of the Sacrament* rely on spectacular bleeding Eucharists and an explosion of the oven in which the unbelieving Jews have tried to incinerate it – a ploy, perhaps, to create a sense of unity among diverse and conflicted Christians by recalling the one group they agree in persecuting, even if that group was still absent from England following Edward I's explusion of the Jews in 1290.

Such drama may seem far from the history plays or tragedy that developed in the Renaissance. Yet whether officially sponsored by the church or by the town guilds, or mounted by professional troops, the medieval religious drama presents bold experiments with the vision of history, and these may establish the foundations of later tragedy. In the York Crucifixion play – produced, with deliberate irony, by the guild of Pinners – the crucifiers are exacting professionals, discussing the technical difficulties of stretching a body and nailing its limbs to the Cross. They manipulate Jesus's living body with no signs of interest in its experience. Their technology, not its results, obsesses them; they epitomize Hannah Arendt's 'banality of evil'. Jesus, meanwhile, in the centre of their business, does not address them either. He is silent for much of the play. Finally, he addresses the audience beyond the cluster of tormenters: 'Biholdes mine heede, mine handis and my feete.' His 'you' joins the immediate town audience viewing him with the expanse of all Christian history, but it also emphasizes his profound isolation from the human beings immediately within his present scene. Although he will have his return in the Last Judgment play, his loneliness in dying is elevated to a universal, trans-historical condition, and it is one that the York townspeople, not God, nor even the clergy, are asked to try to remedy with their sympathetic gaze. There is no easy consolation for this display of human loneliness. Jesus's torturers, for their part, fail to comprehend that their petty concerns maim their own human wholeness as well as his. In their dogged profession-alism, they cannot see even the immediate results of their efforts on the body that the rest of history is invited to behold. They present the urban tradesmen audience of York with a fully contemporary image of itself, not in a naive ignorance of historical realism but in a use of history suggesting the timelessness of society's blindness to individual isolation, and staging that theme, in spite of the sacred importance of the particular moment presented, within a secular frame of reference. The staging of overtly secular history after the Reformation would require decades of development to realize again such moments of tragic intensity.

Following genres, literary traditions and communities through the lens of cultural and political periods or using genre to frame the literary materials through their historical phases offer complementary ways of introducing the devel-opment and variety of medieval English writing. Such materials, however, need to be assessed from yet another angle: by taking stock of the post-medieval views that have framed and continued to frame the Middle Ages and its lit-erature. Our perspective of the Middle Ages is defined by everything that came after it, and it is necessary to survey the history of interest in medieval materials in order to under-stand our position better and see the options we now have.

3

Critical Approaches

Beginning students may feel even more vividly and immediately than seasoned professionals the weight of history that defines medieval literary study. Those who work in the thick of the subject are perhaps less likely to notice how the premises of which works to study, how to approach them and what values to maintain in analyzing them are all part of a particular academic context and set of traditions (or rejection of traditions). Yet all modern readers and scholars of medieval literature have, of course, a vast separation from their subject, and an intimate participation, conscious or not, in the long tradition of studying it. The more fully we understand that history, the better we can define our own terms for managing the distance, and for assessing past and ongoing endeavors.

Medieval literary studies may be cast in three phases. From the Renaissance through the eighteenth century, medieval (and other) English literature was not an academic subject, but a focus of scholars in a wide range of social and professional positions that allowed them to work on such materials, from clerics to royal antiquaries to archivists to lawyers. From the nineteenth century until roughly the last quarter of the twentieth century, medieval literature found a secure, indeed central home in universities, forming a required subject in many university programs. Finally, in more recent decades it has often ceased to be required academic knowledge, but it has gained a much wider array of possible approaches.

Beyond these differences of settings, these involve a host of shifting issues. Surveying them may help us better see the assumptions that have shaped our present position and options, as well as the potential in the material itself to serve so many uses, present and past.

FROM THE RENAISSANCE THROUGH THE EIGHTEENTH CENTURY

The Renaissance

By the early sixteenth century not only had almost all knowledge of the English from Anglo-Saxon England been lost, but also considerable knowledge of even later medieval English pronunciation and thus poetic meter. Many works that we consider the great treasures of medieval English poetry – *Beowulf*, the *Owl and the Nightingale*, the *Pearl* poems, and *Yvain and Gawain*, for instance – were altogether unnoticed. With the Reformation, most medieval writing, in fact, was rapidly redefined as 'papish' (part of the Roman papal church), and treated with a mixture of contempt and longing.

Amid all the changes in language, in the church and in the arrival of the printing press, a sense of a 'former' age is as evident as a 'new' one. Something like the period that we now mark as 'medieval' – from the fall of Rome to the Reformation – was named or conceived by the early seventeenth century by writers like the English antiquarian William Camden (in his *Remaines of a greater worke*, 1605), and the essayist Francis Bacon (who speaks in his *Advancement of learning* [also 1605] of 'the middle part of time', after the fall of Rome: bk. 2, p. 12). Those first collecting the fragments of medieval culture seem particularly aware of an 'age' that had come to an end. John Leland's commission as the 'king's antiquary' in 1533, charging him 'to serche after England's Antiquities and to peruse the libraries of all cathedrals, abbayes, priories, collects, &c', allowed him to note a vast array of medieval books in their original locations. His pursuit eventually was driven by an obsession to visit as many places as he could that he had read about in medieval chronicles and romances, although before he could complete his plan to collect and catalog all the nation's medieval books he went mad – the punishment for assisting the king's heresy, some thought; the price of overwork in scholarship, others believed.

Even a sane antiquary would have found the task of recording medieval England before it vanished daunting. As the monasteries went down after the Acts of Dissolution in 1536 and 1539, often reduced simply to their abbey churches, and church sacraments were redefined and diminished, most of the books vanished into various hands. By the 1560s, the Corpus Christi plays were censored (chiefly for their teachings on the sacraments); by the 1570s they had disappeared. The collective town 'cycle drama' had, however, already been losing popularity to the increasing numbers of plays staged by traveling professional players. Protestantism and capitalism together extinguished the last visible enactment of medieval culture.

Anglo-Saxon English in the Renaissance

For all that they opened the gates of destruction, the Acts of Dissolution also put into new hands a vast range of books that had not been pondered in centuries. Pre-Conquest English first appeared in print in Archbishop Matthew Parker's *Testimonie of antiquitie* (?1566), just as the last Corpus Christi plays were being suppressed. In this small edition of some prose by Ælfric, Parker, who formulated the Thirty-Nine Articles on which Anglican Church doctrine rested, and translated the 'Bishops' Bible' that put forth an official English Bible for the Anglican Church, carefully chose writings to refute the view that Anglican doctrine was 'new doctryne, not knowen of olde in the church' (p. 2). For did not Ælfric's sermon on Easter – the only text Parker printed in full – explain the Eucharist in terms that agreed with Article 28 of the Thirty-Nine Articles, *na swaþeah lichamlic ac gastlice*, 'not so withstanding bodely, but ghostly', as Parker's facing-page translation declared? Lest this blow against Catholic doctrine (in which the Eucharist is both materially and spiritually God) be missed, his note adds 'No transubstantiation' (p. 35). So too the versions of the Lord's Prayer and the Creed in Anglo-Saxon English, which Parker presented as well, showed that presenting scripture 'in the English tounge' was 'no new thyng' (p. 74). He also gathered evidence that Anglo-Saxon priests had sometimes married, supporting Article 32, which Parker himself followed by getting married.

His printing of Anglo-Saxon prose to show the historical depth of the English religion and language set a firmly encouraging pattern for others. More prose was printed, and the 'English-Saxon' language began to be studied. But awareness of Anglo-Saxon English poetry lagged. Substantial amounts of poetry first appeared only with Francis Junius's 1654 Amsterdam edition of the Anglo-Saxon biblical epics *Genesis*, *Exodus*, *Daniel* and *Christ and Satan*, from the book we now call the Junius manuscript – and all of it was attributed to Cædmon himself. But otherwise, the poetry was nearly invisible until the mid-eighteenth century. Edward Thwaites's edition of Ælfric's *Heptateuch* (1698) printed the elegant poetic fragment known as *Judith*, but presented it, like the other materials there, as prose (following more closely than we do now the format of the original manuscript, which like all English poetry of the Anglo-Saxon period presented it like prose). It thus constitutes yet another Saxon translation of the Bible.

Not surprisingly, given this focus, Thwaites completely ignored another poem found in the manuscript of *Judith* and partly written by the same scribe: *Beowulf*. That poem received mention only in 1705, in Humphrey Wanley's catalogue of manuscripts, added to George Hickes's *Linguarum vetussimarum septentrionalium thesaurus grammatico-criticus et archæologicus*: there,

Wanley (in Latin) identified *Beowulf* as a 'most noble poetic treatise'; he quoted a dozen lines in prose form and summarized its subject as 'the wars that a certain Dane, Beowulf, waged against the kings of Sweden' (vol. 2: 218–19). (Apparently Wanley read only the beginning and end.) Not until the Icelandic scholar Grímur Jónsson Thorkelin printed it in 1815 did *Beowulf* gain a wider readership. In part, that reaction was stirred by the sense of outrage that a 'foreigner' had been the first to investigate such an important testimony of ancient English culture.

By then, the medieval past had begun to seem a 'national' heritage worth claiming and quarreling over, as the nineteenth-century debates between German and French scholars about the place of Charlemagne in their two nations' histories show. Medieval literature was valuable almost entirely as an index of its culture, and that in turn as both a foil to and origin of the present world.

Later medieval English in the Renaissance

English poetry from the later Middle Ages generally fared slightly better in the immediate post-medieval centuries. Langland's *Piers Plowman* enjoyed an enthusiastic but vigorously biased reception by Protestants (see Middleton, in Alford 1988: 1–8). Its first editor, Robert Crowley, saw its anticlerical satire as placing its author among those in the 'papish' period who dared 'to open their mouthes and crye oute agaynste the workes of darkenes' (as Crowley says in his 1550 preface). Chaucer, whose influence on fifteenth-century literature was powerful, gained some attention by Puritans (such as John Foxe) eager to find their predecessors in his anti-clerical satire; and, as late as Dryden, Chaucer was considered a supporter of the founder of Lollardy, in part the result of the regular inclusion in *The Canterbury Tales* of *The Plowman's Tale*, an anticlerical screed not by Chaucer. Few scholars could reconcile late medieval poets' intense satire of the clergy with fundamental support of the medieval church – and even now this is difficult for many. On the other side, the poetic works presenting medieval clerical instruction, *Cursor mundi*, the *Pricke of Conscience*, Robert Mannyng's works and others, were wholly ignored.

But Chaucer, and for a time Gower, could be plucked from his immediate world by being valued as the best instances of as urbane or 'liberal' a style as the 'middle age' might offer, as well as a definable founder to anchor the new sense of the English 'literary tradition'. Both Chaucer and Gower had the strong advantage, not shared by Langland or the *Pearl* poet (or of course any earlier writers), of using a dialect of English close to what became the standard Westminster English. Chaucer and Gower had been endorsed by fifteenth-century writers for their 'aureate' ('golden') language, and Chaucer was acclaimed as 'The firste fydere [*inventor*] of our fair langage' (Hoccleve, *Regiment of Princes*, line 4978), a reputation that long continued. But with the changes in English pronunciation, and the silencing of final – which Renaissance writers did not know to sound in his poetry, Chaucer was seen throughout the sixteenth and seventeenth centuries as a primitive forefather because he was capable of only a clumsy metre. 'Ancient Gower' appears in Shakespeare's *Pericles, Prince of Tyre* (1608) to flatter an audience 'born in those latter times, / When wit's more ripe' (I, Prologue, 11–12), from whom he begs pardon for 'the lame feet of my rhyme' (IV, Prologue, 48). To accentuate the effect, Shakespeare renders Gower's lines in halting octosyllabic couplets, and uses the 'modern' iambic pentameter in the rest of his play.

Even John Dryden, whose praise of Chaucer led to a confirmation of the poet as the great founder of English literature, emphasized that 'he lived in the infancy of our poetry, and . . . nothing is brought to perfection at the first' (in the *Preface to Fables Ancient and Modern*, 1700). Dryden, however, offered the most detailed praise so far of Chaucer as literary 'genius'. He emphasized Chaucer's position as translating and adapting sources but found that in this lay his originality: the depiction of 'lively' characters and 'manners: under which name', Dryden says, 'I comprehend the passions and, in a larger sense, the descriptions of persons, and their very habits'. These were also the traits that were generally enshrined from the eighteenth century on as features of a distinctively 'national' English literature.

Anglo-Saxon literature in the eighteenth century

Study of the history of the English language developed through the eighteenth century (see Gneuss 1996). Earlier, Camden's 1605 *Remaines of a Greater Worke* presented the first history of medieval English as a language, sampling various translations of the prayer 'Our Father', from *c.*700 through Chaucer's period. Such interest did not, however, gain a wide following until the nineteenth century, in spite of some more systemic inquiries into the history of the Germanic languages, especially the collection of materials in Hickes' *Thesaurus*.

The language reeked of an alternate, and for many attractively so, political world. The English language of Anglo-Saxon England seemed to offer a compelling guide to quasi-democratic 'Saxon' political values before those fell under the 'Norman Yoke' in 1066. In 1724, an edition of an English text by the fifteenth-century lawyer, Sir John Fortescue, *A Treatise of the Difference between Absolute and Limited Monarchy*, includes an introduction by Sir John's descendant, Sir John Fortescue-Aland, praising the tradition of 'Saxon' law before the Norman Conquest as the oldest and thus the closest to 'the law of Nature'. Fortescue-Aland adds a paean to the earliest 'Saxon tongue' as a key to an informed and well-ordered political community. So transparent were the roots in words that social perceptions were unclouded by French obfuscations: 'one might be tempted to think that the common People, in the Time of the Saxons, understood more than the common People now, or at least were less expos'd to Mistake; because the Words of their Mother Tongue were more comprehensive and scientifical, and less liable to give them wrong Ideas' (p. xliv).

The view that the Anglo-Saxon language brought a sense of a purer political culture was shared by a number of the

American Founding Fathers, especially Thomas Jefferson, who owned a copy of Fortescue-Aland's edition of the *Treatise* on monarchy. Jefferson developed its principles into a lifelong advocacy of learning Anglo-Saxon English and merged this with broader political and cultural ideals. By studying 'Saxon', Jefferson argued, students 'will imbibe with the language their free principles of government' (*Papers*, Memorial Edition, 16.51; see Hauer 1983: 880). The supposed political 'freedom' of 'Saxon England' was claimed on many sides as the French and American revolutionaries stirred into action. In 1771 appeared in London an anonymous *Historical Essay on the English Constitution*, which sought to trace English politics through the entire medieval period to show that 'our Saxon forefathers, have founded their government, upon the common rights of mankind', including 'the elective power of the people' (p. 6) and, Rousseau-like, upon 'considering every man alike, as he came from the hands of his maker, man as man, simply and detached from any foreign advantages, one might, accidentally, have over another' (p. 4) – until they were undone by the oppressive Normans, but were then redeemed by Magna Carta, which allowed them to demand just laws and political representatives. The *Historical Essay* marshals such materials to contribute to a heated public debate about taxing the American colonies. But its agenda finally is that of the British gentry who held that the province of America must not on any account be released from such ancient British parliamentary authority, lest the 'British Empire' itself collapse.

A sly rebuttal to the *Historical Essay* was printed in Philadelphia in 1776 (*The Genuine Principles of the Ancient Saxon, or English Constitution*, signed by 'Demophilus', Greek for 'Lover of the People'), which quotes extensively from the *Historical Essay* but argues that the real originator of the Saxons' oppression was King Alfred, for he established the principles of monarchy that denied the Saxons their rights (a criticism echoed about the same time by the firebrand medieval scholar who supported the French Jacobins, Joseph Ritson 1802: lxix). Instead of Magna

Carta, 'Demophilus' closes with a copy of the American Declaration of Independence.

Such charged uses of Anglo-Saxon history fueled the more scholarly interests that followed the American Revolution – and finally led to sustained interest in the poetry. In 1805 Sharon Turner's *History of the Anglo-Saxons* first appeared by 1836 five more editions had followed, each longer than the last. The first edition briefly mentions *Beowulf*, but the sixth dedicates a long chapter to summarizing and quoting it in translation. This was the pivotal moment in *Beowulf*'s rise to canonicity. Yet just as the late seventeenth century had made Anglo-Saxon English poetry an appendage of religious writing, so the early nineteenth made it an appendage of Anglo-Saxon culture: Turner praises it as a valuable 'exhibition of the feelings and notions of those days' (6th edn., vol. 3: 287).

Thus *Beowulf* emerged in terms of a broad historical inquiry; it was viewed not as a unique poetic artifact but as a transparent vehicle for Anglo-Saxon heroic culture. Not surprisingly, in this perspective it was deemed 'primitive' in literary terms. Like many other thinkers throughout the nineteenth century, Turner viewed history as a story of progress: 'the English fancy was cultivated with assiduous labour for many centuries before Chaucer arose, or could have arisen', Turner remarks (vol. 3: 275). 'Fancy' in this period was a nearly technical term for 'poetic imagination', used regularly to discuss the literary achievements of Shakespeare, Milton, Shelley, Keats, Coleridge and Wordsworth. Even with *Beowulf* before him, Turner's passing comparison to Chaucer assumes the later poet's foundational place in the real 'flowering' of English literature.

Later medieval English literature in the eighteenth century

One sign of Chaucer's position as the 'Homer' of English literature through the eighteenth century was his position at the head of the John Bell's *Poets of Great Britain* (1782), where Chaucer's works fill the first fourteen of Bell's 109 affordable volumes. That position was earned by centuries of considering Chaucer a poet for poetry's sake. Unlike Langland, Chaucer did not seem by this time to take any strong polemical stand on any issues, but remained urbanely wry in all political and social settings; unlike Gower, he did seem to be an apologist for a particular political party. Gower's status dropped after the seventeenth century in part because his direct political commentary against Richard II and his direct support of Henry Bolingbroke in the *Confessio Amantis* and elsewhere (although he first presented those views well before it was expedient to do so) made him seem a political sycophant, an image scorned by eighteenth-century poets. Chaucer's style, in contrast, was politically as well as literarily elusive; his mimicry of the voices of the humble, or of women, allowed later poets to mime his mimicry in turn, with what they took to be a similar kind of knowing detachment and poetic control.

Thus Alexander Pope transformed Chaucer's *The Wife of Bath's Prologue* and *The Merchant's Tale* into fully contemporary eighteenth-century English and style, using Augustan couplets and including pat moral endings, setting those among his 'imitations' of 'the Ancients' whom, he generously allowed, have 'as much Genius as we' (Preface to his *Works* 1717). So too John Gay wrote a witty play, *The Wife of Bath* (1713, revised 1730), built around showing Chaucer besieged by eager poetasters and engaged in wooing a noblewoman with his elegant love poetry. She succumbs to his advances only when she is convinced that he writes his poetry for her – which Gay's Chaucer shows that he does not, since he also composes a lyric against marriage (Act IV, 560 ff.; ed. Fuller 1983, vol. 1: 155), in the vein of the real Chaucer's 'Envoy to Bukton'. The play ends with Chaucer's marriage and his display of 'captivating' the fair Myrtilla with the love poetry that she desires; but it leaves a strong impression of Chaucer's urbane distance from women, inept love poets and inept competing lovers alike.

In the eighteenth century, no other later medieval English author was a comparable model of 'modern' self-possessed and detached wit. At best they were treated as transparent windows to their 'age' and, apart from serving that role, the literary properties that impeded such direct social understanding were dismissed or regarded as repellently exotic. Thomas Warton's huge *History of English Poetry* (1774–81), for instance, whose first volume treats medieval poetry, opens with a 'Dissertation' tracing the 'origins of Romantic fiction' from 'the fictions of Arabian imagination' to the Welsh, from whom Geoffrey of Monmouth derived his stories of King Arthur. Warton presented the fullest survey of medieval English literature so far, quoting a rich quantity of the later medieval English writings that had been nearly or entirely invisible: he discovered the solitary copy of *Ywain and Gawain*, and of the *Pearl* poems (*Pearl, Cleanness, Patience, Sir Gawain and the Green Knight*), and he presented some parts of those for the first time. But he did not even mention *Sir Gawain* (it was not printed until 1839), and, whereas he found Langland praiseworthy for his 'satire on the vices of almost every profession: but particularly on the corruptions of the clergy', he considered that Langland's alliterative metre 'contributed . . . to render his manner extremely perplexed, and to disgust the reader with obscurities' (pp. 266–7).

In predictable contrast to such 'obscure' alliterative writing, Warton finds it easy to show that Chaucer, whose discussion fills six of the eighteen sections of Warton's first volume, has a 'genius' that 'was universal, and adapted to themes of unbounded variety . . . In a word, that he appeared with all the lustre and dignity of a true poet, in an age which compelled him to struggle with a barbarous language, and a national want of taste' (p. 457). Chaucer's talents particularly lay in his 'Characters', which 'are all British, and bear no suspicious signatures of classical, Italian or French imitation' (p. 435). Even the fullest exploration of the 'exotic' Middle Ages could discover in Chaucer a reassuring echo of the present aspirations of literary taste.

While Warton was publishing his volumes, Thomas Tyrwhitt's pioneering edition of *The Canterbury Tales* (1777) appeared, setting the record straight at least on Chaucer's metrical precision and polish, accounting for the final -*e* and other features of late medieval English pronunciation. No equally sympathetic scrutiny of later medieval English alliterative meter was available until the late nineteenth-century editions of *Piers Plowman* by the great editor W. W. Skeat.

FROM THE NINETEENTH THROUGH THE MID-TWENTIETH CENTURY

With the nineteenth century began a more complete division between the popular and scholarly interests in medieval materials that persists to this day. Creative utopian medievalism flourished – novels by Walter Scott (who also edited a number of later medieval English poems, arguing steadily for their Scottish origins); poems by Alfred Lord Tennyson (continuing in the tradition of Dryden and Pope); and a host of projects by William Morris, as editor, designer, artisan, publisher and center of an entire movement of 'Arts and Crafts', based on the ideal of the Middle Ages as based on handmade elegance and beauty rather than mass-produced culture, which was becoming so dominant at this time of the 'Industrial Revolution'. All such fascination could be either nostalgic for an image of a more socially stable and authoritarian hierarchy, or find in medieval literature a socially rebellious alternative to the alienated wage-labor of nineteenth-century industrial capitalism.

At the same time, the academic study of medieval literature began to grow into a central and rigorously scholarly endeavor for studying medieval culture generally. This pursuit was spurred by a sense that it held the 'origins' of modern, nationalist culture. If popular views sought a Middle Ages as escape from modern life, scholarly views sought it as a foundation to modernity. Germany was the center of the new industry of 'Germanic philology', the study of the family of languages that ultimately flowered (as this perspective assumed) in modern German itself, but which included medieval English as an offshoot that had been increasingly corrupted by 'outside' influences (see Utz 2002). Jacob Grimm (better known for his and his brother's collection of fairy tales, which express the same basic value for 'folk culture') helped transform Germanic linguistics with his *Deutsche Grammatik* (1819–37), which presents a comprehensive overview of the Germanic languages. Later scholars made significant advances in understanding the Anglo-Saxon English language and, finally, alliterative meter; in 1893 Eduard Sievers presented his scheme of five basic patterns of Anglo-Saxon English verse that remains the starting point for all discussions of its meter, even those that seek to supplement its principles (Cable 1991).

The idea of Germanic culture, in this age of Wagner and Nietzsche, inspired the pursuit of an original Germanic paganism, and English as well as German scholars sought to identify – and sometimes to omit – those parts of Anglo-Saxon English literature that had been 'corruptly' added to the 'original' pagan elements of the poetry, as 'Christian colouring' (Blackburn 1897; see Stanley 1975). Lines overtly praising Christianity in *Beowulf* (lines 186–9), and in *The Seafarer* (lines 64 ff.), were marked as later additions. The general view persisted into the twentieth century; when Ezra Pound published his translation of *The Seafarer* in 1911, he omitted all lines from the poem mentioning or implying Christianity – a translation still offered as an authentic version of Anglo-Saxon poetry.

This approach was not comprehensively challenged until Frederick Klaeber argued in 1912 that the Christian elements were fundamental parts of that as well as every English poem from Anglo-Saxon England, a view sustained in his great edition of *Beowulf* first appearing in 1922 (the third edition of 1950 has remained continuously in print). This ultimately led to a far more complex assessment of *Beowulf* (see, e.g., Whitlock 1951), and to interest in a wider range of Anglo-Saxon literary production, with greater awareness of its pervasive poetic sophistication.

In literary studies of later medieval English writing, other major endeavors to define the 'origins' of modern England gradually helped found the entire academic field of English literary study. The industrious Frederick J. Furnivall founded the Early English Text Society in part to supply the words for another major project conceived in 1857 that he had taken charge of, the New English Dictionary (later renamed as the Oxford English Dictionary when a more secure publisher, and a more steadily attentive editor, were found). This dictionary sought – and still seeks – to trace the historical meanings of all English words in use after 1050. Furnivall, a Christian Socialist, saw later medieval English literature as 'the poor man's classics'; to edit such works was a democratic and patriotic labor, as well as a contribution to linguistic and literary history. Furnivall also founded the Chaucer Society in 1867, and scholarly and student editions of that poet began to appear on all sides.

The tradition of treating Chaucer's poetry in more purely 'literary' terms than other medieval English writers did not cease even in this increasingly dense literary environment. George Lyman Kittredge, whose engaging lectures on Chaucer (1915) seem inspired by his sense of Chaucer's own wit, focused on some of the key poetic elements that, in shifting terms, remained central in Chaucer criticism through at least the next half century. Chaucer is a master of irony, Kittredge emphasized, and of dramatic presentation – indeed his work presents a kind of drama (a view extended later); he has a 'strong sense of fact' in all of his use of literary conventions. He is particularly gifted at creating character: 'the Wife of Bath is one of the most amazing characters that the brain of man has ever yet conceived' (p. 189). Some of Kittredge's views, such as his approval of Pandarus as 'a rare but perfectly human compound of enthusiasm and critical acumen' (p. 139), began to seem faded only by the 1970s and 1980s, when the focus on Pandarus, and Chaucer himself, started to attend more critically to how women were portrayed as the objects of male attention.

Through the 1950s and 1960s Chaucer, in opposition to other medieval writers, remained a focus of 'literary' analysis that, like the New Critics by which it was inspired, such as

I. A. Richards, W. K. Wimsatt, William Empson and others, sought ways to appreciate his 'style' and satiric ambiguities rather than assess any social viewpoint or bias in his perspective (see Middleton 1992). Even 'Chaucerians' (a specialist category that hardly exists anymore) did not relinquish historical orientations entirely. The most important mid-twentieth century 'New Critical' study of Chaucer, by Charles Muscatine (1957), deftly focused on Chaucer's blend of realism, satire and dissonant levels of 'style', but did so in terms of the broad claims of medieval literary history current in the early twentieth century, especially those of W. P. Ker (1912, continually in print until 1945), who saw the 'native' English tradition as reinvigorated by the French literary tradition. In the 1960s, a deliberate 'historicist' opposition was mounted to what were seen as the 'romantic' values foisted upon Chaucer, in the form of a newly ambitious use of theological context. The 'exegetical' scholar D. W. Robertson Jr (e.g. 1962) argued that the long-influential Christian theological principles of Augustine's notions of 'charity' and 'cupidity' shaped medieval literature in general and Chaucer in particular, either directly as in didactic literature, or indirectly as in ironic depictions of sinfully cupidinous characters. In this view, medieval literature was almost always either ironic or allegorical, and, as the vigorous opponents to this strategy claimed, almost never directly appreciated 'just as literature'. Here, the Middle Ages was seen as decisively different from the modern world, and any suggestion that modernity began there was viewed as anachronistic.

A more detailed and scholarly pursuit of Christian meanings and images soon focused on detailed source study. This continued the philological tradition more than the 'exegetical' tradition, as Robertson and his followers defined that, and it also sought to show that literary 'meaning' was better available by way of very particular Christian allusions and contexts. In these terms, R. E. Kaske (see the list of his works in Kaske 1988: xxi–xxiii) and his followers opened medieval English literary scholarship onto a large realm of Latin, and sometimes other non-English, Christian materials in pursuit of textual sources and analogues for vernacular literature. Such work helped bring literature into a domain of 'medieval studies' as a broad intellectual and cultural region, moving medieval literary studies toward the more varied connections to cultural context that, impelled by other trends in literary studies generally, soon began to dominate.

CURRENT ISSUES AND DEBATES

Medieval literary scholars from the 1970s on have not ignored the theological traditions of the 'exegetical' scholars, but they have also increasingly been presented with other options for thinking about literature as part of medieval culture. In many branches of literary scholarship, more anthropological and cultural kinds of analysis of literature and 'discourse' emerged from feminist theory, cultural theory and a range of Marxist-influenced social views that were influencing or redefining formalist and structuralist criticism, and which, after a slower process of assimilation than in other fields, by the 1980s began to do so in medieval literary study as well.

The heated debates in scholarship about the importance of theological contexts to medieval literature were, in fact, not settled but eclipsed by the broader questions about context posed by culturally oriented 'theory'. Medieval scholars seemed particularly well positioned to take these up – even while they often reveal an aversion to applying to medieval literature something so obviously 'modern' as the language and philosophical lineages of 'theory'. 'What is an author?' Foucault asked; and medievalists showed that they could see far better than Foucault himself how medieval literature, with its very different sense of authorship, might at least indirectly answer that question. 'How does an encounter with social authority define the self?' a range of Marxist theorists from Louis Althusser to Raymond Williams asked; and again medievalists showed that they were in a position to pursue that point in distinctive ways. A series of feminists, from Gayle Rubin to Julia Kristeva, asked 'What are the images and functions of women?'; and medievalists could pursue a wide range of relatively unstudied materials and new perspectives on well-known ones. Foucault's further questions, 'What is the history of sexual identity, and how have the idea of sexuality and its repression defined the self?' also provoked medieval scholarship, spurred by the interest of a time before modern sexual categories were fully defined.

While medievalists rarely framed their studies directly around the questions and concepts of modern theorists (for some exceptions, see Frantzen 1991, Cohen 2000), many of these questions from 'theory', especially cultural theory, can be seen as general background to a number of pursuits in medieval scholarship from the late 1970s through the 1990s and beyond. In a general or specific way, as inspiration or rebuttal, they help define such topics as the medieval academic ideas of authorship (Minnis 1984), the socially defined ideas of writers' authority and relations to their publics (Middleton 1978, 1982, 1990), the notion of the self and how particular kinds of social authority generally were mediated by literature and history writing (Aers 1988, Patterson 1991, Justice 1994), and the categories of medieval sexual identity and the visions of women (Carruthers 1979, Dinshaw 1989 and 1999, Hanson 1992, Frantzen 1996, Dinshaw and Wallace 2003, and many others).

Anglo-Saxon English literature more slowly and infrequently received similar consideration, in terms that sought to elucidate literary narrative through cultural structures, including but not limited to those of gender (e.g. Overing 1990, Earl 1994, Howe 1989 and 1997). More prominent in placing Anglo-Saxon English poetry in a cultural as well as literary historical context were the emphatic claims from the late 1980s on for an 'oral formulaic' poetics. Such a view has roots in much earlier scholarship, such as the second edition of MacPherson's *Works of Ossian* (1775), but its technical application to medieval literary formulas and type-scenes began in Homeric studies with Milman Parry's research on oral poets in Yugoslavia (modern Kosovo) in the 1920s, then appeared in studies by Albert Lord in 1960s, followed by work on Anglo-Saxon English and other Germanic literatures by Alain Renoir (1988) and John Miles Foley (e.g. 1991), work that continues to the present (see Niles 1999, Amodio 2004). This approach challenges those who sought exclusively textual lineages or narrowly literary or political contexts for the poetry; it approached poetic 'meaning' and 'art' by defining these as part of a vast and now almost unavailable context of associations and type-scenes.

Scholarship on English in Anglo-Norman England has usually remained closer to direct historical and philological study, but it has begun expanding its ambitions in tying these more to literary effects (e.g. Donoghue 1990, Galloway 2006). A significant interest in writings for women such as the 'Katherine Group' have begun to grow, and some projects on medieval constructions of gender have attended to the *Ancrene Wisse*, the work written by a male confessor to help a group of women anchoresses fashion their lives (Millett and Wogan-Browne 1990, Bartlett 1995).

Although medieval philosophy sometimes viewed the properties of language as the key to virtually every other important reality, there was curiously little effort to use the theories of 'deconstruction' to tease out issues in medieval literature concerning oppositions between 'real' and 'representation', 'essential' and 'supplementary', and 'writing' and 'speech', oppositions which were put under provocative pressure in the writings of Jacques Derrida and others. Instead, deconstruction itself was placed in a new role: it was applied to culturally oriented arguments about medieval literature and other writing (Leicester 1987 and, less directly, 1990, Gellrich 1995). Even with that generally non-contextual set of tools and questions, medievalists have continued to contribute to cultural history in some form.

Study of medieval drama, which was established with monumental surveys of the development of vernacular drama (Chambers 1903) and Latin liturgical drama (Young 1933), both cast in essentially 'evolutionary' terms, shifted first to closer scrutiny of the immediate theological context and import of the Corpus Christi drama (Kolve 1966), then to a sharp focus on medieval staging and immediate historical contexts of production (Nelson 1974), detailed pursuit of which continues in the 'Records of Early English Drama' series. More recently such inquiry has bridged 'performance' with cultural 'performativity', and expanded the definition of drama to public displays of all kinds (e.g. Emmerson 1990, Paxson, Clopper and Tomasch 1998, Nisse 2005).

Study of later medieval English other than Chaucer has sought to formulate how literary histories of particular regions may be uncovered beneath the effects of Chaucer's obscuring reputation (Hanna 2005); *Piers Plowman* in particular has been used to understand a relation between particular moments in the later fourteenth century and the literary or other strategies used to support or transform those (e.g. Justice and Kerby-Fulton 1997). Study of romances and Malory has developed into a rich range of inquiry into the representations of texts, authorship, gender, violence, identity and social order (e.g. Batt 2002). These issues are somewhat similar to those currently pursued for other late medieval English literature, but romance has also received attention for its distinctive role in literary culture, such as the communal circulation and mobile reappearance of its motifs or 'memes' (Cooper 2004), or how the particular manuscripts of these invariably anonymous works continually redefine the genre and the representation of such materials (Evans 1995, Jacobs 1995).

Chaucer studies have used his writing as a key to the cultural modes of his London world, in contact with the very different modes and contexts of the Italian literature that he used so insistently (Wallace 1997). Chaucer's preeminent status is no longer openly bolstered, but instead scrutinized as a phenomenon, a key to the literary and cultural postures of later English and even American culture (Lerer 1993, Trigg 2002, Prendergast 2004, Carlson 2004, Barrington 2006). In an increasing context of reflection on the traditions of medieval scholarship, study of 'medievalism' in literary and scholarly history has flourished (e.g. Frantzen 1990, Matthews 1999, Simmons 2001, Ganim 2005).

The results of such dense connections between literary or narrative capability and cultural outlooks, contexts and modes of power are more often richer histories or kinds of connections than in easily transportable new theoretical concepts. Where students and scholars in later periods can assume some basic historical contexts, those in medieval literature must sometimes be the first to establish and explore, or significantly reformulate them (e.g. Hudson 1988, Justice 1994, Strohm 1998). The demands on knowledge can be intense, and some trade-offs are inevitable. Language and source-study are generally less stressed as the chief key to medieval literary inquiry now than through the first half of the twentieth century; contextual inquiry and analytical ingenuity are all the more important. The training that might yield 'authoritative editions' – study of linguistics, dialects, scribal 'corruption', reconstructing the lost originals, determining the sources and analogues – has also less often been sustained. Yet other aspects of medieval textual studies have made extraordinary gains in scope and visibility, especially attention to how individual manuscripts fit their contexts and shape the 'genres' and 'forms' of medieval literature. Scholars pursuing all manner of issues have turned to the immediate moment, or layers of moments, of a work's social moment and material 'presence' in medieval copies, read, used and remade for particular purposes (e.g. Hanna 1997, Bryan 1999).

As all this shows, the historical situating of medieval literature has certainly not disappeared, but it has changed focus to engage immediate social contexts more deeply and to look around or 'under' some of the most traditionally monumental figures or traditions. At the same time, medieval literary history has focused increasingly on the question, 'How does medieval English literature matter now?' (e.g. Frantzen 1990, Niles 1997, Biddick 1998, Dinshaw 1999, Strohm 2000, Trigg 2002, Ganim 2005.) The question is not pursued prescriptively, as in how it *ought* to matter. Rather, it is usually posed with a full commitment to the period itself but also a self-conscious sense that the past is always framed in response to the preoccupations and needs of the periods of those responding to it, including the present.

The focus on what 'matters now' is perhaps also a reaction to the increasingly vast array of available materials. As Chaucer and even *Beowulf* have shifted away from the positions of supreme attention, there is an embarrassment of riches and an exciting but daunting number of texts to master. Student editions of materials in late medieval English pour forth from the TEAMS series; EETS continues to issue two or more crucial scholarly editions a year; editions of Anglo-Saxon English writing proliferate; and translations of medieval works not in English continue to appear. Many of these are also available on the Internet – not to mention the major series of medieval Latin texts whose vast contents are now being converted to digital and thus searchable forms, for those who know Latin, which is therefore more than ever a critical skill: the *Patrologia Latina*, the *Corpus Christianorum*, and the *Monumenta Germaniae Historiae*.

With astonishing numbers of reproductions of medieval manuscripts available in microfilm, CD-ROM and, increasingly, the Internet, the reasons *not* to study the works in their 'original' form are disappearing. So too, the reasons to avoid consulting early printed books have also evaporated, with access of those appearing via the Internet too. Such databases democratize one of the traditionally most exclusive aspects of scholarly research; anyone with access to a library that subscribes to these projects can make a home office into an enormous rare book room. All of the books printed before 1800 mentioned in this book were read by this means.

Amid all these materials and approaches, guidance is more important than ever, for students and scholars alike. Conferences, very local or international, are as important to scholars as classrooms are to students; encounters between and across many disciplines and languages are all the more important, since the categories of 'cultural history' have extended so broadly. Facing the materials and options to which we are heir, we may feel ourselves uniquely aware that no one can 'master' the vast range of medieval literature and culture, as seems expected for a modern scholarly field. Still less can we settle the questions of its continuities and differences from the periods that follow, an issue that in some form continues to frame such materials. Yet the impossibility of mastery remains one of the enduring fascinations of this vast, alien, but sometimes, and unpredictably, intimately present and meaningful span. Accepting our role as explorers, testing new skills and ideas against the materials and pondering how our questions reveal our own present circumstances and needs are usually the best ways to start discovering important and interesting things in any domain. Certainly these are the best ways to enter this realm of English literature and culture, as we trace connections that we did not think to discover and hear a past speak that we did not expect to understand.

4

Resources for Independent Study

CHRONOLOGY OF KEY HISTORICAL AND CULTURAL EVENTS

Key concepts, defined below and discussed in previous chapters, are indicated in bold.

c.311   Conversion to Christianity of Constantine the Great, Emperor of Rome (*c.*272–337)

354–430   St Augustine, Bishop of Hippo in North Africa: author of hundreds of works, most influentially *The City of God*; *The Confessions*; *On Christian Doctrine*; and the *Soliloquiae*

5th c.   Western regions of the empire overrun by Germanic invaders

?480–524   Anicius Manlius Severinus Boethius, Christian Roman statesman and philosopher, translator of many works by Aristotle and author of the vastly influential *Consolation of Philosophy*

597   Mission of St Augustine of Canterbury (monk with the same name as the earlier bishop and saint)

	from Rome to Thanet, Kent, to introduce Roman Christianity to England.
657–80	*Caedmon's Hymn*
7th–8th c.	*Dream of the Rood*
c.730	Ruthwell Cross, Dumfries, Scotland (inscribed with some of the text found in *Dream of the Rood*)
731	Completion of *The Ecclesiastical History of the English People* by Bede, monk of Wearmouth-Yarrow monastery, Northumbria, author (among many works) of commentaries on the Bible, works on the calendar, and the *Life of St Cuthbert* (in prose and verse)
742–814	Reign of Charlemagne, first ruler of the Christian western empire
? 8th c.–11th c.	*Beowulf* (epic poem)
8th–9th c.	*Exodus* (epic religious English poem)
9th c.	Cynewulf's poems: *Elene*; *Fates of the Apostles*: *Juliana*; *Andreas*
865	First major Viking incursion into England
878	Treaty of Wedmore (creation of Danelaw)
890–9	The *Preface* and *Epilogue* to Alfred's translation of Gregory the Great's *Pastoral Care*
10th c.	English *Blickling Homilies*
937	Battle of Brunanburh (event and poem)
991	Battle of Maldon (event and poem)
c.1000	Ælfric, *Homilies*
c.1015	Wulfstan, *Homilies*
c.1050	*Chanson de Roland*, French epic (earliest copy *c.*1150)
1066	Norman Conquest
1070–1126	William IX of Aquitaine, first troubadour
1086	Domesday Book, a detailed survey of the properties and communities through much of England ordered by William I, for uncertain purposes
1096–9	First Crusade

1098	St Anselm of Canterbury, *Cur deus homo* ('Why God as human'), influential account of the logic of the incarnation of God as Jesus
c.1124– 1204	Eleanor of Aquitaine; literary patron and granddaughter of William IX of Aquitaine; wife of King Louis VII of France (marriage annulled); wife of Henry II of England
1132	Abelard, *Historia calamitatum*
1137	Geoffrey of Monmouth, *History of the Kings of Britain* (first full account of King Arthur)
1139	Gratian, *Concordia discordantium canonum* (first full collection of canon law)
1146–8	Second Crusade
c.1150– 65	French 'ancient romances' written in England: *Roman de Thèbes*; *Roman d'Eneas*; Benoît de St Maure's *Roman de Troie*
c.1150– 1200	French romances of Chrétien de Troyes
1154	*Peterborough Chronicle*, last continuation of The *Anglo-Saxon Chronicle*, comes to an end
1155	Wace, *Brut*, French verse translation of Geoffrey of Monmouth's Latin *History of the Kings of Britain*
1155–72	Henry II's controversy with Thomas Beckett (murdered 1170)
1167	Oxford organized as a *studium generale* (on the model of the University of Paris)
c.1170	*Lais* of Marie de France
c.1170– 80	Alan of Lille: *Plaint of Nature*, and *Anticlaudianus* (Latin allegorical works influential on much vernacular literature)
1187–92	Third Crusade
1194	Richard I captured and ransomed on crusade
c.1200	*Owl and the Nightingale* (English poem)
1215	Magna Carta ('great charter'), formulated by the barons to constrain the king in taxation, justice and feudal rights; later taken as general proclamation of subjects' legal rights Fourth Lateran Council (in Rome) issues series of

canons governing the clergy's guidance of the laity, including the obligation for all lay-folk to confess their sins to a priest at least once a year (canon 21), and requiring Jews and 'Saracens' (Muslims) to wear a badge indicating their difference from Christians (canon 68)

c.1220 *Ancrene Riwle* (or *Ancrene Wisse*)
Layamon, *Brut*; first account in English of King Arthur

c.1225 'Katherine group' of English saints' lives and homiletic writings: *Sawles Weard*; *Life of St Katherine*; *Life of St Margaret*; *Hali Meithhad*

c.1225–50 'Tremulous Hand' glosses Anglo-Saxon English homiletic and grammatical manuscripts

c.1235 Guillaume de Lorris (in Orléans, France) writes first part (to line 4059) of *Roman de la Rose*, a poetic love allegory

c.1275 Jean de Meun (in Orléans, France), continues Guillaume de Lorris's *Roman de la Rose* as a long satirical and allegorical narrative

c.1275–1300 Bodleian Library MS Digby 86 (important collection of French and English religious and secular poetry and prose)

c.1280 *South English Legendary* (collection of saints' lives)

1285 Conquest of Wales by Edward I

1290 Expulsion of Jews from England by Edward I

1290–1349 Richard Rolle, mystical prose and poetry

c.1300 *Havelok*; *Cursor mundi*; *The Chronicle of Robert of Gloucester*

1304–74 Francesco Petrarca (Francis Petrarch), Italian intellectual and poet

c.1308–38 Robert Mannynge: *Handlynge Synne*; *Chronicle of England*

1313–75 Boccaccio (Italian prose writer; author of *The Decameron*)

1314 Battle of Bannockburn

1314–20 Dante, *Divina Commedia*

1327–52	Higden, *Polychronicon* (one of the last Latin universal histories; widely copied and influential in England)
1329–1426	Thomas Hoccleve, poet, translator and scribe; associate of Chaucer; member of the king's Privy Seal office
c.1330	British Library MS Harley 913 (important Anglo-Irish manuscript of satiric and lyric poetry in English and Latin, including the 'Land of Cokayne')
c.1330–40	The Auchinleck Manuscript (National Library of Scotland Advocates MS 19.2.1), (important collection of romances, saints' lives, and other historically oriented materials and narratives)
1337–1410	Jean Froissart, poet and chronicler
c.1340	British Library MS Harley 2253 (important collection of lyrics in French, Latin and English)
1340–99	John of Gaunt, first duke of Lancaster, father of Henry IV, wife of Blanche, later of Katherine Swynford, sister-in-law of Geoffrey Chaucer; probable patron of Chaucer and John Gower
1349	First appearance in England of the Black Death Ordinance of Laborers (law requiring wages of laborers and artificers to return to levels before the Black Death); reissued 1362, 1378 and 1388, the last with rules against vagrancy
c.1350	*Pricke of Conscience* (English poem presenting dogma and moral theology)
c.1360	*William of Palerne* (earliest datable poem in the alliterative revival)
c.1369	Chaucer, *Book of the Duchess*
c.1370	William Langland, *Piers Plowman*, A version
1372–3, 1378	Chaucer's two journeys to Italy
c.1375	John Barbour, *The Bruce*
1376	Good Parliament
c.1379	*Piers Plowman*, B version

1380	Cecily Chaumpaigne releases Geoffrey Chaucer from the charge of *raptus* (either 'rape' or 'abduction')
c.1380– 1400	Wycliffite translation of the Bible
1381	Peasants' Rebellion
1382	John Wyclif condemned for heresy in the 'Earthquake' Council in London
c.1386	Chaucer, *Troilus and Criseyde*
1387	John Trevisa translates Higden's *Polychronicon* Thomas Usk, *Testament of love*
1388	'Merciless Parliament', in which a group of higher nobility convict many of Richard II's counselors on charges of treason. Thomas Usk (author of *Testament of Love* and fan of Chaucer) executed. Chaucer departs London for Kent
c.1388	*Piers Plowman*, C version
c.1389	Chaucer, The *Legend of Good Women* (revised *c.*1395)
c.1390	Bodleian Library, Oxford, MS. Eng. poet. a.1 (the Vernon MS): large collection of didactic English prose and poetry, including the earliest copy of the A version of *Piers Plowman*
c.1390–8	John Gower, *Confessio Amantis*
c.1390– 1400	Chaucer, *Canterbury tales* Alliterative poems: *Siege of Jerusalem*; *Wars of Alexander*; *Sir Gawain and the Green Knight*; *Pearl*; *Cleanness, Patience*
1391– 1447	Duke Humphrey, youngest son of Henry IV and major patron of poets, including John Lydgate
1400	Death of Chaucer
1400–2	In France, Christine de Pizan, Jean Gerson, Jean de Montreuil and the Brothers Col (Pierre and Gontier) exchange letters debating the morality of the *Roman de la Rose*, in what becomes known as *La querelle de la Rose* ('The debate about the *Rose*')
1400–9	Revolt of Owain Glyn Dŵr, Welsh lord, against Henry IV

1401	*De heretico comburendo*, English statute authorizing the burning of recalcitrant heretics
1410	Disendowment Bill (Lollard knights' presentation of a bill in parliament to have the monasteries stripped of all lands)
	John Badby burned as a Lollard
	Thomas Hoccleve, *Regimen of Princes*, a 'mirror for princes' dedicated to Prince Henry, later Henry V
1413	Julian of Norwich, *Showings* (short text; long text was written some time later)
1414	Revolt by Sir John Oldcastle (Lollard knight)
1415	Battle of Agincourt
c.1415	*Castle of Perseverance* (moral play)
1420	John Lydgate, *Troy Book*
1421	John Lydgate, *Siege of Thebes*
c.1423	Thomas Hoccleve, *Compleinte and Dialog*
1430–5	John Lydgate, *Fall of Princes*
1431	Henry VI crowned king of France. Jeanne d'Arc burned
c.1436	*Book of Margery Kempe*
1450	Rebellion of Jack Cade
1453	English lose France (except Calais)
1455–85	Families holding titles of Lancaster and York contend over the throne, in the War of the Roses
1456	End of Hundred Years War (1339–1456)
1461	Henry VI, insane, is deposed
c.1465	*Mankind* (moral and satirical play)
	Croxton Play of the Sacrament
c.1470	Blind Harry, *The Wallace* (long poem on Scottish hero)
	Sir Thomas Malory, *Le Morte d'Arthur*
	Robert Henryson, poems
c.1474	Caxton prints *Dicts and Sayings of the Philosophers* (first book printed in England)
c.1477	Caxton prints Chaucer's *The Canterbury Tales*
c.1500	William Dunbar, poems

Glossary of Key Terms and Concepts

Acts of Dissolution
The two Acts passed by Parliament (1536, 1539) to dissolve English monasteries and return their properties to the Crown, on the supposed grounds of general moral turpitude and treason; after popular protests and some temporary refoundations of monasteries, the royal commissioners carrying out the Acts expelled all monks or persuaded them to surrender their properties, leading many to depart England to establish 'recusant' communities in France and Switzerland, where many Catholic translations of medieval Latin texts were published.

Allegory
Writing that uses personifications of ideas or abstract entities ('Nature' or 'Holy Church'); also, narratives whose literal events are offered, or are later read as offering, coded assertions about virtues, ethics or other claims (e.g. David's seduction of Bathsheba in 2 Samuel 11 is to be understood as Jesus' conversion of the soul). See also Chapter 2.

Alliterative poetry, alliterative revival
Poetry using initial stressed consonants and vowels, often divided into two half lines, usually having alliteration on the first three main stresses; with variations, the style is common in Germanic and Celtic literatures, and nearly universal in English poetry from Anglo-Saxon England. The appearance of a new burst of English poetry based on this metrical

principle from *c.*1360, and less actively continuing through the fifteenth century, has drawn various explanations, from oral continuities with earlier traditions to the remaking of a poetry based on alliterative homiletic prose; see also Chapter 2.

Anglo-Latin literature

Latin literature written in England between *c.*600 and *c.*1500. Such writing, present in vast quantities and with continuous literary vitality, ranges from the allegorical to the satiric, from the topical to the saintly, and includes the most important historical writing of the Middle Ages (see Rigg 1992).

Anglo-Norman literature

French literature written in England between *c.*1150 and *c.*1500, and often in the distinct French dialect of the Normans, including romance, lyric, allegory, saints' lives and chronicles.

Black Death

The widespread, easily transmissible and usually quickly fatal disease that appeared in the 1340s in Europe and England, perhaps brought in by returning crusaders, and killing up to half the population. The plague continued to return in waves through the sixteenth century.

Canon law

The written set of laws used by the church and first collected in 1139 by Gratian, which governed all clerical activity of any kind and all activity by the laity that pertains to morals or theology; its matters were judged in church courts (or 'Court Christian') that were legally separate from the king's or local lords' courts.

Continuation, historical or literary

Additions to chronicles or to literary works, rarely involving any changes to the preceding sections but rather extending the work as a collaborative project, with the continuator's role sometimes explicitly stated and sometimes merely inferable from changes in style or other evidence.

Crusades

A series of military efforts by western Christian kings, rulers, hermits and even common people to conquer the Muslims occupying Jerusalem, beginning in 1096 and continuing into the early fifteenth century, although few of the many plans for major assaults were put into practice after 1270, the last major crusade (by St Louis, King of France).

Danelaw

Northern and eastern counties governed by the Danes who had settled in the England during the ninth and early tenth centuries after the assaults of the Vikings; the region was divided in 878 from Wessex by a line running diagonally east and north from above London, and was mostly re-conquered by the English in the later tenth century.

Dogma and moral theology

Basic and unchallengeable information about belief, including sacred cosmology and history, and the nature of vice and virtue.

Epic

Long, historical poem centered on a hero's military triumphs in the service of a larger social and historical goal. See Chapter 2.

Germanic

Pertaining to the many peoples and the genetically related languages of Western Europe (English, German, Norse, Gothic, Frisian, etc.), especially during the period of Roman colonization and contact (1st century BC–5th century AD).

Heresy, heretic

Based on the Greek for 'choice', heresy refers to a belief or set of beliefs that accept the basic deity worshiped in an orthodox or officially accepted religion but differ in crucial details of worship or institutional loyalty from the views officially accepted when observing that religion. Thus Lollards agreed, for instance, that the Eucharist became 'substantially' the body and blood of God upon consecration, but, against orthodox views, maintained that 'accidentally', in its material elements, it remained bread and wine; they also agreed that confession to God was a sacrament, but disagreed that this needed a priest; they agreed that the true church was the body of those who were saved, but disagreed that the institutional church deserved support as the manifestation of the true church.

King Arthur
Supposed king of England descended from Brutus, son of Aeneas (founder of Rome), whose rule in the fifth century was said to extend through Europe and indeed to include Rome. Fragmentary materials of Arthur and some battles appear in ninth- through twelfth-century writing from Wales, and possibly much of his legend derives from there, but in the form known the stories most derive from the Latin chronicle of Geoffrey of Monmouth (*c*.1137).

Lay-folk, laity
All those not in clerical orders. The term, when not otherwise specified, often indicates a social status below aristocratic.

Lyric poetry
Short, often explicitly personal poetry, often about a beloved, human or divine, and often expressing the speaker's desires and efforts to attain that beloved, or the speaker's sense of loss, personal or universal. See also Chapter 2.

Mirror for princes
Compendious works presenting public advice to princes of the virtues that they should cultivate, based on the widely known *Secretum Secretorum* (ninth century from an Arabic original, and widely translated) and reaching to Machiavelli's *Prince*.

Monk, monastic
Based on the Greek word for 'solitary', hence 'apart' (from the world), a *monacus*, in Western Europe, is one who dwells

in a monastery under an abbot and following the Rule of St Benedict (c.530), which prescribes a strenuous routine of daily prayer, sacred song and pious readings and sometimes writings (often including the recording of history).

Mystical prose

Prose, common in England in the fourteenth and fifteenth century, euphorically extolling love for God or describing visions of God, usually including some form of religious instruction to readers as well as the speaker's own sense of transport.

Nobility

Land-owning families and individuals with lineages possessing long-standing power and prestige. The process of separating the status of knights, nobles and higher nobles unfolded progressively from the twelfth century on. In the later fourteenth century, the category of the 'higher nobility', the 'peers of the realm', became more clearly distinct from the lesser nobility, and new ranks of nobility continued to be created through the sixteenth century.

Patron, literary

Wealthy and powerful supporter of a poet or other writer or performer, who might be a member of the patron's household or a more occasional beneficiary of the patron's financial and social support. 'Publication' in medieval culture often involved presenting a formal copy of a work to a patron, whose endorsement would serve to publicize the work and who sometimes would make available the work for others to copy.

Privy Seal, office of

Branch of the king's civil service created in the eleventh century, originally directly attached to the king but by the fourteenth century a separate office in the complex bureaucracy linking the king, his secretary and the secretary's Signet Office, Chancery, the King's Council and any interested parties who had sought a writ from the royal bureaucracy. The Privy Seal was responsible for issuing and 'sealing' royal documents from the mundanely local to the crucially international; by the late fourteenth century it was staffed with literate laymen rather than clerics.

Romances

Narrative poems, often historically oriented but also often including magical elements, and usually focused on love lost and recovered, within a larger social world.

Saints' lives

Narratives of the lives and, often, the violent deaths of saints, and often including the miracles associated with their body or grave or relics, or simply the worship of them, after their death. See also Chapter 2.

Satire

Direct or ironic criticism of social or, less often, individual abuses, as measured by overt or implied ideals, a common medieval literary mode. See also Chapter 2.

Secular

Usually, to do with non-religious experiences, actions and endeavors (from Latin *saeculum*, 'age', 'period' of worldly history); can be applied either to literary issues or materials or to the laity's way of life. But secular priests are simply priests who live among the laity, rather than monks or other conventual religious who are also ordained as priests (allowed to administer the sacraments to lay-folk).

Troubadours

Writers and performers of lyric love poetry in southern France, in French and Occitan flourishing from the twelfth through the fourteenth centuries, possibly influenced by Arabic poetry, and in turn influencing much European poetry.

Universal history

Chronicles or narrative works tracing the history of the world from Creation to the present, widely popular from the twelfth century through the early fourteenth.

Viking

Marauders traveling by sea from Iceland and Denmark during the warm months in the ninth century to attack and pillage coastal monasteries and other settlements; by the eleventh century their settlement in Normandy (from 'Norseman') founded by the Viking Rollo (d. 932) established a major, thoroughly Christian duchy.

Historical Table of Kings and Rulers

(— = sibling or half-sibling; | = son)

ANGLO-SAXON KINGS

'Bretwalds' or otherwise prominent early kings, with centers in various kingdoms

ÆLLE, King of the South Saxons, r. approx. 477–91

CEAWLIN, King of the West Saxons, r. approx. 560–93

ÆTHELBERT, King of Kent, r. approx. 560–616

RÆDWALD, King of East Anglia, r. approx. 590–620

EDWIN, King of Northumbria, r. approx. 616–32 (killed)
OSWALD, King of Northumbria, r. 633–41
—OSWIU, King of Northumbria, r. 641–70

ÆTHELBALD, King of Mercia, r. 716–57
OFFA, King of Mercia, r. 757–96

WEST SAXON KINGS

EGBERT, r. 802–39
|
ÆTHELWULF, r. 839–55

|
ÆTHELBALD, r. 855–60
—ÆTHELBERHT, r. 860–6

|
—ÆTHELRED I, r. 866–71
—ALFRED, r. 871–99

|
ÆDWARD, r. 899–925

|
ÆTHELSTAN, r. 925–39
—EADMUND I, r. 940–6 (murdered)
| —EADRED, r. 946–55

|
EADWY, r. 955–9
—EADGAR, r. 959–75

|
EADWARD II, r. 975–9 (murdered)
—ÆTHELRED II, 'the Unready' (i.e. 'ill-advised'), r. 979–1016
| —EADMUND II, 'Ironside', r. 1016
| |
| (Svein Forkbeard)
| |
| CNUT, king of England and Denmark, r. 1017–35
| |
| HAROLD I, r. 1035–40
| —HARDACNUT (CNUT II), r. 1040–2
|
EADWARD III, 'the Confessor', r. 1047–66

(Earl Godwin)
|
HAROLD II, r. 1066 (killed)

ANGLO-NORMAN KINGS

WILLIAM I, King of England and Duke of Normandy, r. 1066–87

|
WILLIAM II, r. 1087–1100
—HENRY I, r. 1100–35
(—Adela)
|
   STEPHEN, r. 1135–54; 'The Anarchy'

LATER MEDIEVAL KINGS

(Geoffrey, Count of Anjou and Maine; conquered duchy of
Normandy from Stephen)
|
HENRY II, r. 1154–89
|
RICHARD I, r. 1189–99
—JOHN, r. 1199–1216
|
HENRY III, r. 1216–72
|
EDWARD I, r. 1272–1307
|
EDWARD II, r. 1307–27 (murdered)
|
EDWARD III, r. 1327–78
| |
| (Edward of Woodstock, 'The Black Prince')
| |
| RICHARD II, r. 1378–99 (deposed)
|
(John of Gaunt, Duke of Lancaster)
|
HENRY IV, r. 1399–1413
|
HENRY V, r. 1414–22
|
HENRY VI, r. 1422–61 (deposed)

(Richard Plantagenet, Duke of York; great-grandson of
EDWARD III by Edmund of Langley, Duke of York)

|

EDWARD IV, r. 1461–83

|

EDWARD V, proclaimed king 1483, never crowned
(murdered)
—RICHARD III, brother of Edward IV, r. 1483–5 (killed in
battle)

(Owen Tudor, second husband of Henry V's widow,
Katharine of France)

|

(Edmund Tudor, Earl of Richmond [d. 1456], husband of
Margaret Beaufort [d. 1509], who was great-granddaughter
of John of Gaunt by his third wife, Katherine Swynford [d.
1403])

|

HENRY VII, r. 1485–1509

|

HENRY VIII, r. 1509–53

References and Further Reading

HISTORICAL, CULTURAL AND INTELLECTUAL CONTEXTS

General histories

Blair, P. H. (1977) *An Introduction to Anglo-Saxon England* (2nd edn). Cambridge: Cambridge University Press.

Clanchy, M. T. (1998) *England and its Rulers 1066–1272* (2nd edn). Oxford: Blackwell.

Holt, J. C. (1972) *Magna Carta and the Idea of Liberty*. New York: John Wiley.

Keen, M. (1990) *English Society in the Later Middle Ages 1348–1500*. Harmondsworth: Penguin.

Rigby, S. H. (ed.) (1988) *A companion to Britain in the later Middle Ages*. Oxford: Blackwell.

Stenton, F. M. (1971) *Anglo-Saxon England* (3rd edn). Oxford: Clarendon Press.

Whitelock, D. (1952, 1984) *The Beginnings of English Society*. Harmondsworth: Penguin.

The church and clerical culture

Armstrong, R. J., Hellman, J. A. W. and Short, W. (eds and trans.) (1999–2002) *Francis of Assisi, Early Documents*, 3 vols. New York: New City Press.

Constant, G. (1966) *The Reformation in England: The English Schism and Henry VIII 1509–1547*. New York: Harper & Row.

Duffy, E. (2005) *The Stripping of the Altars: Traditional Religion in England, c.1400–c.1580* (2nd edn). New Haven, CT: Yale University Press.

Gilson, E. (1955) *History of Christian Philosophy in the Middle Ages*. New York: Random House.

Kretzmann, N., Kenny, A. and Pinborg, J. (eds) (1982) *The Cambridge History of Later Medieval Philosophy*. Cambridge: Cambridge University Press.

Oberman, H. A. (1983) *The Harvest of Medieval Theology: Gabriel Biel and Late Medieval Nominalism*. Durham, NC: Labyrinth Press.

Pantin, W. A. (1963) *The English Church in the Fourteenth Century*. Notre Dame, IN: University of Notre Dame Press.

Swanson, R. N. (1989) *Church and Society in Late Medieval England*. Oxford: Blackwell.

Books and literacy

Clanchy, M. T. (1993) *From Memory to Written Record, England 1066–1307* (2nd edn). Oxford: Blackwell.

Griffiths, J. and Pearsall, D. (eds) (1989) *Book-production and Publishing in Britain, 1375–1475*. Cambridge: Cambridge University Press.

Knights and the aristocracy

Duby, G. (1980) *The Three Orders: Feudal Society Imagined*, trans. A. Goldhammer. Chicago: University of Chicago Press.

Keen, M. (1984) *Chivalry*. New Haven, CT: Yale University Press.

Laborers and the economy

Dobson, R. B. (1983) *The Peasants' Revolt of 1381* (2nd edn). London: Macmillan.

Faith, R. (1997) *The English Peasantry and the Growth of Lordship*. London: Leicester University Press.

Postan, M. M. (1972) *The Medieval Economy and Society*. Harmondsworth: Penguin.

History of English

Blake, N. F. (1996) *A History of the English Language*. New York: New York University Press.

Smith, J. J. (1996) *An historical Study of English: Function, Form and Change*. London: Routledge.

LITERATURE, ANGLO-SAXON ENGLAND

Guides

Chase, C. (ed.) (1981) *The Dating of Beowulf*. Toronto: University of Toronto Press.

Donoghue, D. (2004) *Old English Literature: A Short Introduction*. Oxford: Blackwell.

Orchard, A. (2003) *A Critical Companion to Beowulf*. Rochester, NY: D. S. Brewer.

Language textbooks and anthologies

Marsden, R. (2004) *The Cambridge Old English Reader*. Cambridge: Cambridge University Press.

Mitchell, B. and Robinson, F. C. (2001) *Guide to Old English* (6th edn). Oxford: Blackwell.

Pope, J. C. (ed.) (2001) *Eight Old English Poems* (3rd edn, rev. R. D. Fulk). New York: Norton.

Whitelock, D. (1992) *Sweet's Anglo-Saxon Reader in Prose and Verse* (15th edn). Oxford: Clarendon Press.

Anthologies of texts in translation

Bradley, S. (trans.) (1982) *Anglo-Saxon Poetry*. London: Dent.

Swanton, M. (trans.) (1975) *Anglo-Saxon Prose*. London: Dent.

Swanton, M. (trans. and ed.) (1996) *The Anglo-Saxon Chronicle*. London: Dent.

Keynes, S. and Lapidge, M. (ed. and trans.) (1983) *Alfred the Great: Asser's Life of King Alfred and Other Contemporary Sources*. Harmondsworth: Penguin.

Editions of poetry

Chickering, H. D., Jr (ed. and trans.) (1977) *Beowulf: A Dual-language edition*. Garden City, NY: Anchor Books.

Klaeber, F. (1922, 1950) *Beowulf and the Fight at Finnsburg* (1st edn, 3rd edn). Lexington, MA: D. C. Heath.

Mitchell, B., and Robinson, F. C. (eds) (1998) *Beowulf: An Edition*. Oxford: Blackwell.

Individual editions of other Old English poems abound, too numerous to list here. The standard collected edition of all the poetry (but with no glossary or grammatical notes), grouped by the medieval 'book' in which it appears but excluding the prose that also appears in those medieval books, is as follows:

Krapp, G. P. and Dobbie, E. V. K. (eds) (1931–5) *The Anglo-Saxon Poetic Records*, 6 vols. New York: Columbia University Press.

Selected editions of prose

Bately, J. (ed.) (1980) *The Old English Orosius*. Oxford: Oxford University Press.

Bethurum, D. (ed.) (1957) *The Homilies of Wulfstan*. Oxford: Clarendon Press.

Carnicelli, T. (ed.) (1969) *King Alfred's Version of St Augustine's Soliloquies*. Cambridge, MA: Harvard University Press.

Clemoes, P. (ed.) (1997) *Ælfric's Catholic Homilies: The first series text*. Oxford: Oxford University Press.

Crawford, S. J. (ed.) (1922) *The Old English Version of the Heptateuch. Ælfric's Treatise on the Old and New Testament and His Preface to Genesis*. London: Oxford University Press. Reprinted with additions by N. R. Ker, 1969.

Godden, M. (ed.) (2000) *Ælfric's Catholic Homilies: The second series text*. Oxford: Oxford University Press.

Pope, J. C. (ed.) (1967–8). *Homiles of Ælfric: A supplementary collection*, 2 vols. London: Oxford University Press.

Scragg, D. G. (ed.) (1992) *The Vercelli Homilies and Related Texts*. Oxford: Oxford University Press.

ENGLISH LITERATURE IN ANGLO-NORMAN AND LATER MEDIEVAL ENGLAND

Guides
(see also 'Critical approaches' below and Chapter 3)

Alford, J. A. (ed.) (1988) *A Companion to Piers Plowman*. Berkeley: University of California Press.

Barney, S. (2006) *The Penn Commentary on Piers Plowman, Volume 5 C Passus 20–22; B Passus 18–20*. Philadelphia: University of Pennsylvania Press.

Brown, P. (2000) *A Companion to Chaucer*. Oxford: Blackwell.

Burrow, J. A. (1971) *Ricardian Poetry: Chaucer, Gower, Langland and the 'Gawain' poet*. New Haven, CT: Yale University Press.

Galloway, A. (2006) *The Penn Commentary on Piers Plowman, Volume 1: C Prologue–Passus 4; B Prologue–Passus 4*. Philadelphia: University of Pennsylvania Press.

Pearsall, D. (1992) *Life of Geoffrey Chaucer: A critical biography*. Oxford: Blackwell.

Putter, A. (1996) *An Introduction to the Gawain-poet*. New York: Longman.

An ongoing series of bibliographies and basic information on various Middle English genres and authors is available in *A Manual of the Writings in Middle English, 1050–1500*, New Haven: Connecticut Academy of Arts and Sciences, 1967–2005 to date (11 vols).

General anthologies

Bennett, J. A. W. and Smithers, G. V. with a glossary by Norman Davis (ed.) (1974) *Early Midddle English Verse and Prose* (2nd edn). Oxford: Clarendon Press.

Burrow, J. A., and Turville-Petre, T. (ed.) (2005) *A Book of Middle English* (3rd edn). Oxford: Blackwell.

Dickins, B., and Wilson, R. M. (ed.) (1969) *Early Middle English Texts*. London: Bowes and Bowes.

Gray, D. (ed.) (1988) *Late Medieval Verse and Prose*. Oxford: Oxford University Press.

More focused anthologies

Romances

Sands, D. (ed.) (1986) *Middle English Verse Romances*. Exeter: University of Exeter Press.

Shepherd, S. H. A. (ed.) (1995) *Middle English Romances*. New York: Norton.

Lyrics

Brown, C. (ed.) (1932) *English Lyrics of the XIIIth Century*. Oxford: Clarendon Press.

Brown, C. (ed.) (rev. G. V. Smithers) (1965) *Religious Lyrics of the XIVth century* (2nd edn). Oxford: Clarendon Press.

Duncan, T. G. (ed.) (1995) *Medieval English Lyrics, 1200–1400*. Harmondsworth: Penguin.

Duncan, T. G. (ed.) (2000) *Late-medieval English Lyrics and Carols, 1400–1530*. Harmondsworth: Penguin.

Gray, D. (ed.) (1992) *English Medieval Religious Lyrics*. Exeter: University of Exeter Press.

Robbins, R. (ed.) (1952) *Secular Lyrics of the XIVth and XVth Centuries*. Oxford: Clarendon Press.

Robbins, R. (ed.) (1959) *Historical Poems of the XIVth and XVth centuries*. New York: Columbia University Press.

Drama

Bevington, D. (compiler) (1975) *Medieval Drama*. Boston: Houghton Mifflin.

Coldewey, J. (ed.) (1993) *Early English Drama*. New York: Garland, 1993.

Walker, G. (ed.) (2000) *Medieval Drama: An anthology*. Oxford: Blackwell.

Other

Barr, H. (ed.) (1993) *The Piers Plowman Tradition*. London: Dent.

Millett, B., and Wogan-Browne, J. (ed.) (1990) (see below under 'Critical approaches').

Turville-Petre, T. (ed.) (1989) *Alliterative Poetry of the Later Middle Ages: An anthology*. Washington, DC: Catholic University of America Press.

Individual texts

EETS, the Early English Text Society (scholarly but with full glossaries), and TEAMS, Kalamazoo's Medieval Institute's Consortium for teaching medieval literature (oriented to students), present the widest range of editions of early and later Middle English texts, in poetry, prose and drama. These are too numerous to list here. EETS is generally more authoritative, but some older EETS editions are now superseded by TEAMS or other editions. Other important or useful editions in neither series are as follows:

ANGLO-NORMAN PERIOD

Barron, W. R. J. and Weinberg, S. C. (ed. and trans.) (1989) *Layamon's Arthur: The Arthurian section of Layamon's Brut*. Exeter: University of Exeter Press.

Cartlidge, N. (2001) *The Owl and the Nightingale: Text and translation*. Exeter: University of Exeter Press.

Clark, C. (ed.) (1970) *The Peterborough Chronicle, 1070–1154* (2nd edn). Oxford: Clarendon Press.

LATER MEDIEVAL PERIOD

Chaucer

Barney, S. A. (2006) *Troilus and Criseyde [by] Geoffrey Chaucer*. New York: Norton.

Benson, L. D. (gen. ed.) (1987) *The Riverside Chaucer* (3rd edn). Boston: Houghton Mifflin.

Langland

Kane, G., Donaldson, E. T. and Russell, G. (eds) 1988–97. *Piers Plowman* (rev. edn). 3 vols (A, B and C Version). London: Athlone; Berkeley: University of California.

Pearsall, D. (ed.) (1994) *William Langland: Piers Plowman, the C-text*. Exeter: Exeter University Press.

Schmidt, A. V. C. (ed.) (1995) *Piers Plowman: A parallel-text edition, Volume I: Text.* London: Longman.

Schmidt, A. V. C. (ed.) (1995) *William Langland: The vision of Piers Plowman: A critical edition of the B-text* (2nd edn). London: Dent.

The *Piers Plowman Electronic Archive* is reproducing on CD-ROM all of the manuscripts of the poem with various choices of presentation, and will eventually create a full and manipulatable critical edition of all three versions of the poem. Updated information is available at www.iath.virginia.edu/seenet/piers/

Other late medieval English texts

Andrew, M. and Waldron, R. (eds) (2002) *The Poems of the Pearl Manuscript: Pearl, Cleanness, Patience, and Sir Gawain and the Green Knight.* Exeter: University of Exeter Press.

Ellis, R. (ed.) (2001) *'My compleinte' and Other Poems: Thomas Hoccleve.* Exeter: University of Exeter Press.

Morris, R. (ed.) (1863) *The Pricke of Conscience (Stimulus conscientiae). A Northumbrian poem by Richard Rolle de Hampole.* Berlin: For the Philological Society, by A. Asher. (The poem is not by Rolle but this remains the only edition.)

Perryman, J. (1980) *The King of Tars.* Heidelberg: Carl Winter Universitätsverlag.

Important editions of Middle English prose other than those in EETS and TEAMS

Babington, C. and Lumby, T. (eds) (1865–86). *Polychronicon Ranulphi Higden monachi Cestrensis: Together with the English translations of John Trevisa and of an unknown writer of the fifteenth century,* 9 vols. London, Longman.

Knight, I. K. (ed.) (1967) *Wimbledon's Sermon: Redde rationem villicationis tue; A Middle English sermon of the fourteenth century.* Pittsburgh, PA: Duquesne University Press.

Sargent, M. (ed.) (1992) *Nicholas Love's Mirror of the Blessed Life of Jesus Christ.* New York: Garland.

Shepherd, S. H. A. (ed.) (2004) *Le morte Darthur, or, The hoole book of*

Kyng Arthur and of his noble knyghtes of the Rounde Table. New York; Norton.

LITERARY AND OTHER PRIMARY MATERIALS ONLINE

The Auchinleck Manuscript: www.nls.uk/auchinleck/ index.html
Early English Books Online (printed books to 1700; subscription only): http://eebo.chadwyck.com/home
Eighteenth-Century Collections Online (subscription only): www.gale.com/EighteenthCentury/
Internet Medieval Sourcebook www.fordham.edu/halsall/sbook.html
Labyrinth, Georgetown: http:www.georgetown.edu/labyrinth/
Middle English compendium, University of Michigan (subscription only): www.hti.umich.edu/mec/
Old English materials: www.engl.virginia.edu/OE/
Teams Middle English texts: www.lib.rochester.edu/camelot/teams/tmsmenu.htm
Wessex Parallel Webtexts (Middle English lyrics): www.soton.ac.uk/~wpwt/
Wulfstan's *Sermon of the Wolf:* http://english3.fsu.edu/~wulfstan/

CRITICAL APPROACHES AND LITERARY SCHOLARSHIP (DISCUSSED IN CHAPTER 3)

Adams, E. N. (1970 [1917]). *Old English Scholarship in England from 1566–1800.* Hamden, CT: Archon.
Aers, D. (1988) *Community, Gender, and Individual Identity: English writing, 1360–1430.* London: Routledge.
Amodio, M. C. (2004) *Writing the Oral Tradition: Oral poetics and literate culture in medieval England.* Notre Dame, IN: University of Notre Dame Press.
Anon. (1771) *Historical Essay on the English Constitution.* London: Edward and Charles Dilly.
Bacon, F. (1605) *The Two Bookes of Francis Bacon: Of the proficience and advancement of learning, divine and humane.* London: Henry Tomes.

Barrington, C. (2006) *American Chaucer*. New York: Palgrave.

Bartlett, A. C. (1995) *Male Authors, Female Readers: Representation and subjectivity in Middle English devotional literature*. Ithaca, NY: Cornell University Press.

Batt, C. (2002) *Malory's Morte Darthur: Remaking Arthurian tradition*. New York: Palgrave.

Bell, J. (ed.) (1782) *The Poetical Works of Geoffrey Chaucer*. Edinburgh: At the Apollo Press.

Biddick, K. (1998) *The Shock of Medievalism*. Durham, NC: Duke University Press.

Blackburn, F. A. (1897) 'The Christian coloring in *Beowulf*', *Publications of the Modern Language Association* 12 (2): 205–55.

Bryan, E. J. (1999) *Collaborative Meaning in Medieval Scribal Culture: The Otho Layamon*. Ann Arbor: University of Michigan Press.

Cable, T. (1991) *The English Alliterative Tradition*. Philadelphia: University of Pennsylvania Press.

Camden, W. (1605) *Remaines of a greater worke, concerning Britaine. . . .* London: Simon Waterson.

Carlson, D. (2004) *Chaucer's Jobs*. Houndmills, Hampshire: Palgrave.

Carruthers, M. (1979) 'The Wife of Bath and the painting of lions', *Publications of the Modern Language Association* 94: 209–22.

Chambers, E. K. (1903) *The Mediaeval Stage*, 2 vols. Oxford: Oxford University Press.

Cohen, J. J. (ed.) *The Postcolonial Middle Ages*. New York: St Martin's Press.

Cooper, H. (2004) *The English Romance in Rime: Transforming motifs from Geoffrey of Monmouth to the death of Shakespeare*. Oxford: Oxford University Press.

'Demophilus' (1776) *The Genuine Principles of the Ancient Saxon, or English Constitution*. Philadelphia: Robert Bell.

Dinshaw, C. (1989) *Chaucer's Sexual Poetics*. Madison, WI: University of Wisconsin Press.

Dinshaw, C. (1999) *Getting Medieval: Sexualities and communities, pre- and postmodern*. Durham, NC: Duke University Press.

Dinshaw, C., and Wallace, D. (eds) (2003) *The Cambridge Companion to Medieval Women's Writing*. Cambridge: Cambridge University Press.

Donoghue, D. (1990) 'Layamon's ambivalence', *Speculum* 65: 538–44.

Earl, J. W. (1994) *Thinking about Beowulf*. Stanford: Stanford University Press.

Emmerson, R. K. (1990) *Approaches to Teaching Medieval English Drama*. New York: The Modern Language Association of America.

Evans, M. J. (1995) *Rereading Middle English Romance: Manuscript Layout, Decoration, and the Rhetoric of Composite Structure*. Montreal: McGill-Queens University Press.

Fisher, J. H. (1965) *John Gower: Moral philosopher and friend of Chaucer*. London: Methuen.

Foley, J. M. (1991) *Immanent Art: From structure to meaning in traditional oral epic*. Bloomington: Indiana University Press.

Fortescue, J. (1724) *A Treatise of the Difference Between Absolute and Limited Monarchy* (ed. and intro. J. Fortescue-Aland). London: Bowyer.

Frantzen, A. J. (1990) *Desire for Origins: New language, old English, and teaching the tradition*. New Brunswick, NJ: Rutgers University Press.

Frantzen, A. J. (ed.) (1991) *Speaking Two Languages: Traditional disciplines and contemporary theory in medieval studies*. Albany: State University of New York Press.

Frantzen, A. (1996) 'The disclosure of sodomy in *Cleanness*', *Publications of the Modern Language Association* 111(3): 451–64.

Fuller, J. (ed.) *John Gay: Dramatic works*, 2 vols. Oxford: Clarendon Press.

Galloway, A. (2006) 'Layamon's gift', *Publications of the Modern Language Association* 121(3): 717–34.

Ganim, J. (2005) *Medievalism and Orientalism: Three essays on literature, architecture and cultural identity*. Houndmills, Hampshire: Palgrave.

Gellrich, J. M. (1995) *Discourse and Dominion in the Fourteenth Century: Oral contexts of writing in philosophy, politics, and poetry*. Princeton: Princeton University Press.

Gneuss, H. (1996) *English Language Scholarship: A survey and bibliography from the beginnings to the end of the nineteenth century*. Binghamton, NY: Medieval and Renaissance Texts and Studies.

Grimm, J. (1819–37). *Deutsche Grammatik*, 4 vols. Göttingen: In der Dieterichschen Buchhandlung.

Hanna, R. *London Literature, 1300–1380*. Cambridge: Cambridge University Press.

Hanson, E. T. (1992) *Chaucer and the Fictions of Gender*. Berkeley: University of California Press.

Hauer, S. R. (1983) 'Thomas Jefferson and the Anglo-Saxon language', *Publications of the Modern Language Association* 98 (5): 879–98.

Howe, N. (1989) *Migration and Mythmaking in Anglo-Saxon England*. New Haven, CT: Yale University Press.

Howe, N. (1997) 'Historicist approaches', in O'Keefe, K. (ed.), *Reading Old English texts*. Cambridge: Cambridge University Press, pp. 79–100.

Hudson, A. (1988) *The Premature Reformation: Wycliffite texts and Lollard history*. Oxford: Clarendon Press.

Hurd, R. (1762) *Letters on Chivalry and Romance*. London: A. Millar.

Jacobs, N. (1995) *The Later Versions of Sir Degarre: A study in textual degeneration*. Oxford: Society for the Study of Medieval Languages and Literature.

Justice, S. (1994) *Writing and Rebellion: England in 1381*. Berkeley: University of California Press.

Justice, S. and Kerby-Fulton, K. (eds) (1997) *Written Work: Langland, Labor, and Authorship*. Philadelphia: University of Pennsylvania Press.

Kaske, R. E. with Groos, A. and Twomey, M. W. (1988) *Medieval Christian Literary Imagery: A guide to interpretation*. Toronto: University of Toronto Press.

Ker, W. P. (1912) *English Literature; Medieval*. New York: H. Holt.

Kittredge, G. L. (1915) *Chaucer and his Poetry*. Cambridge: Harvard University Press.

Klaeber, F. (1912) 'Die christlichen Elemente im *Beowulf*', *Anglia* 35: 111–36, 249–70, 453–82; 36: 169–99.

Kolve, V. A. (1966) *The Play Called Corpus Christi*. Stanford, CA: Stanford University Press.

Langland, W. (1550) *The Vision of Pierce Plowman, Now First Imprinted by Roberte Crowley*. London.

Lees, C. A. (1999) *Tradition and Belief: Religious writing in late Anglo-Saxon England*. Minneapolis: University of Minnesota Press.

Leicester, H. M., Jr (1987) 'Oure Tonges *Différance*: Textuality and Deconstruction in Chaucer', in Finke, L. A. and Shichtman, M.

B. (eds). *Medieval Texts and Contemporary Readers*. Ithaca, NY: Cornell University Press, pp. 15–26.

Leicester, H. M., Jr (1990) *The Disenchanted Self: Representing the subject in the Canterbury Tales*. Berkeley: University of California Press.

Lounsbury, T. (1892) *Studies in Chaucer: His life and writings*, 3 vols. New York: Harper.

MacPherson, J. (1775) *Works of Ossian, the Son of Fingal*, 2 vols. London: T. Becket and P. A. Dehondt.

Matthews, D. (1999) *The Making of Middle English, 1765–1910*. Minneapolis: University of Minnesota Press.

Middleton, A. (1978) 'The idea of public poetry in the reign of Richard II', *Speculum* 53: 94–114.

Middleton, A. (1982) 'The audience and public of *Piers Plowman*', in D. A. Lawton (ed.) *Middle English Alliterative Poetry and its Literary Background*. Suffolk: D. S. Brewer, pp. 101–23, 147–54.

Middleton, A. (1990) 'William Langland's "kynde name": authorial signature and social identity in late fourteenth-century England', in Patterson, L. (ed.) *Literary Practice and Social Change in Britain, 1380–1530*. Berkeley: University of California Press, pp. 15–82.

Middleton, A. (1992) 'Medieval Studies', in Greenblatt, Stephen and Gunn, Giles (eds) *Redrawing the Boundaries: The transformation of English and American literary studies*. New York: Modern Language Association, pp. 12–40.

Millett, B. and Wogan-Browne, J. (eds) (1990) *Medieval English Prose for Women: Selections from the Katherine group and Ancrene wisse*. Oxford: Clarendon Press.

Minnis, A. J. (1984) *Medieval Theory of Authorship: Scholastic literary attitudes in the later Middle Ages*. London: Scolar Press.

Muscatine, C. (1957) *Chaucer and the French Tradition*. Berkeley: University of California Press.

Niles, J. D. (1997) 'Appropriations: A concept of culture', in Frantzen, A. J. and Niles, J. D. (eds) *Anglo-Saxonism and the Construction of Social Identity*. Gainesville: University Press of Florida, pp. 202–28.

Niles, J. D. (1999) *Homo narrans: The poetics and anthropology of oral literature*. Philadelphia: University of Pennsylvania Press.

Nisse, R. (2004) *Defining Acts: Drama and the politics of interpretation in late medieval England.* Notre Dame, IN: University of Notre Dame Press.

Overing, G. R. (1990) *Language, Sign, and Gender in Beowulf.* Carbondale: Southern Illinois University Press.

Parker, M. (ed.) [1566?] *A Testimonie of Antiquitie: Shewing the auncient fayth in the Church of England touching the sacrament of the body and bloude of the Lord here publikely preached, and also receaued in the Saxons tyme, aboue 600 yeares agoe.* London: Iohn Day.

Patterson, L. (1987) *Negotiating the Past: the Historical understanding of medieval literature.* Madison: University of Wisconsin Press.

Patterson, L. (1991) *Chaucer and the Subject of History.* Madison: University of Wisconsin Press.

Paxson, J. J., Clopper, L. M. and Tomasch, S. (eds) (1998) *The Performance of Middle English Culture: Essays on Chaucer and the drama in honor of Martin Stevens.* Cambridge: D. S. Brewer.

Pearsall, D. (1992) *The Life of Geoffrey Chaucer.* Oxford: Blackwell.

Pope, A. (1717) *The Works of Mr Alexander Pope.* London: W. Bowyer, for J. Tonson.

Prendergast, T. (2004) *Chaucer's Dead Body: From corpse to corpus.* New York: Routledge.

Renoir, A. (1988) *A Key to Old Poems: The oral-formulaic approach to the interpretation of West-Germanic verse.* University Park, PA: Pennsylvania State University Press.

Rigg, A. G. (1992) *A History of Anglo-Latin Literature 1066–1422.* Cambridge: Cambridge University Press.

Ritson, J. (1802) *Ancient Engleish Metrical Romanceës.* London: Bulmer.

Robertson, D. W., Jr (1962) *A Preface to Chaucer; Studies in medieval perspectives.*

Sievers, E. (1893) *Altgermanische metrik.* Halle, M. Niemeyer.

Simmons, C. A. (ed.) (2001) *Medievalism and the Quest for the 'Real' Middle Ages.* London: Frank Cass.

Stanley, E. G. (1975) *The Search for Anglo-Saxon Paganism.* Cambridge: D. S. Brewer.

Strohm, P. (1998) *England's Empty Throne: Usurpation and the language of legitimation, 1399–1422.* New Haven, CT: Yale University Press.

Strohm, P. (2000) *Theory and the Premodern Text.* Minneapolis: University of Minnesota Press.

Trigg, S. (2002) *Congenial Souls: Reading Chaucer from Medieval to post-modern*. Minneapolis: University of Minnesota Press.

Turner, S. (1836) *History of the Anglo-Saxons, from the Earliest Period to the Norman Conquest* (6th edn), 3 vols. London: Longman *et al.*

[Tyrwhitt, T. (ed.)] (1777) *The Canterbury tales of Chaucer, to which are added an essay upon his language and versification . . .*, 4 vols. London: T. Payne.

Utz, R. (2002) *Chaucer and the Discourse of German Philology: A history of reception and an annotated bibliography of studies, 1793–1948*. Turnhout: Brepols.

Wallace, D. (1997) *Chaucerian Polity: Absolutist lineages and associational forms in England and Italy*. Stanford, CA: Stanford University Press.

Wallace, D. (ed.) (1999) *The Cambridge History of Medieval English Literature*. Cambridge: Cambridge University Press.

Warton, T. (1774) *The history of English poery, from the close of the eleventh to the commencement of the eighteenth century . . . .* London: J. Dodsley *et al.*

Whitelock, D. (1951) *The Audience of Beowulf*. Oxford, Clarendon Press.

Young, K. (1933) *The Drama of the Medieval Church*, 2 vols. Oxford: Clarendon Press.

Zacher, S. and Orchard, A. (eds) (2006) *New Readings on the Vercelli Book*. Toronto: University of Toronto Press.

Index

The index includes topics, medieval authors, anonymous works, historical events, and individuals mentioned in the text (apart from the appendixes). Mentions of modern scholars are included only when their approaches to medieval literature are the subject of discussion (as in chapter three). Mentions of kings and rulers of England, and of queens and queen consorts, are grouped under those categories.